I0108211

it's ALL about LOVE

One Groovy Chick's Journey to Grace

Carrie Blair

it's ALL about LOVE
One Groovy Chick's Journey to Grace

Copyright © 2016 by Carrie Goheen Blair

This title is also available as an ebook and an audiobook.

All rights reserved. This book or any portion thereof may not be reproduced or used in any manner whatsoever without the prior written permission of the author except for the use of brief quotations in a book review.

All Scripture quotations, unless otherwise indicated, are taken from the Holy Bible, New International Version®, NIV®. Copyright ©1973, 1978, 1984, 2011 by Biblica, Inc.™ Used by permission of Zondervan. All rights reserved worldwide. www.zondervan.com The "NIV" and "New International Version" are trademarks registered in the United States Patent and Trademark Office by Biblica, Inc.™
Scripture taken from the New King James Version®. Copyright © 1982 by Thomas Nelson. Used by permission. All rights reserved.
Scripture quotations from THE MESSAGE. Copyright © by Eugene H. Peterson 1993, 1994, 1995, 1996, 2000, 2001, 2002. Used by permission of NavPress. All rights reserved. Represented by Tyndale House Publishers, Inc.

Every effort has been made to give proper credit for all stories and quotations. If for any reason proper credit has not been given, please notify the author and proper notation will be given on future printings.

First Printing, 2016

Carrieblair.net Publishing
Lubbock, Texas
www.carrieblair.net

Printed in the United States of America

What folks are saying...

Carrie is loving, caring, and thoughtful, yet straightforward and helpful by telling the truth in an easy sort of way. She gives with love from her heart! –Debbie Coday

Carrie lives out her faith. –Ronnie Ledbetter

My favorite of Carrie's stories said *love* to me. What spoke to my heart so vividly was how her words gave praise and glory to our God...and I was drawn to honor Him as well.
– Peggy Center

Her words are powerful and are always spoken softly, kindly and with love. – Sue Wells

Carrie inspires me to be a better wife, mother, Christian and human (being) through her leadership. – Carla Thrash

Carrie is one of the most motivational and easy to listen to speakers I have ever heard. She is always sharing (her stories) and inspiring her audience. – Jill Crandall

Good cook, great mom; she raised me and I turned out awesome. -- Favorite Child

Dedicated to the strongest, bravest woman I know –
my mother, Twila Pickrell.
Her unfailing love has always been and
will always be my first great gift.

Mission: Show love, extend grace, and give courage
with a groovy attitude.

Contents

Introduction – They Call Me Potato Chip - 1

I Was Born at a Very Young Age - 7

The Driver of That Baby Blue Pickup is Mine - 15

No More Sleeping in on Sundays - 25

Get Real - 31

Hello, My Name is Carrie, and I'm a Control Freak - 39

My Big 'ol Rock - 47

There is Something in the Water - 55

I'm a Quitter - 59

Iron Sharpens Iron - 65

Sing and be Happy - 75

You Know that You're My Favorite - 87

Try to be Ugly - 97

Obligatory Slop - 107

What's Up With the Words Written in Red? - 113

Washing His Feet With My Tears - 119

Time Out in a 32' Travel Trailer - 129

Handy Dandy Instructions for Cheerful Giving - 139

Pray. Love. Forgive. - 147

If I'd Known I Was Going to Live This Long,
I Would've Taken Better Care of Myself - 163

Put Me in, Coach - 173

But, God! - 179

Outrageous Love, Extravagant Grace, Boundless Joy - 185

Until We Meet Again - 193

Acknowledgments

I thank my husband and kids for believing in me and offering encouragement. Steve, Ashley, Matt, Josh, Jonathan, Shannel and Jacob - you had the power to make or break this dream of mine. I'm grateful for your love and your inspiring stories. Truly, you all motivate me to be a better person every single day.

To De'on Miller, Patricia Verett, Wanda Dyess, Monica Henry, Jana Anderson, and Stephen Cox - Thank you for making bold critiques and offering advice for improvements. This manuscript and my skills are better for your guidance. Iron sharpens iron, indeed.

Leisha Womble – Thank you for providing speaking opportunities, critiquing my presentations and being the one who said, "You have to write a book." Then, after reading the first draft saying, "You left out too much. Keep going." Thank you for believing in the mission and for being such a wildly flamboyant friend. Why be ordinary, right?

Sharlan Proper – Your musical gifts have always amazed me. Thank you for speaking scripture into my life and for revealing a ministry vision for me when I had no clue where to start.

Thank you to my buddy, Kirk Noles, at Everyman Media Works for doing whatever it took to make me look good on the web and on the bookshelf.

That groovy red '66 Chevelle on the cover is courtesy of Jim and Connie Gullette. Thank you for sharing it with me.

The amazing back cover photo of the sunshine bursting through the clouds was taken by Eddie Wimberly. Thanks!

To one of my high school teachers: As a student of yours, I was an enthusiastic writer, and you had been a big fan of my work. As an adult, I brought my elementary-aged kids into your classroom to meet you. You asked if I was still writing, to which I replied, "No, I'm raising kiddos and working." Your comment that day was, "What a waste." The stories in this book are a result of those years. I like to think that my talent wasn't wasted; it was merely marinating.

I saved the best for last: I give all the praise to God. This book is His. I pray that He uses it for His glory and to touch lives. Yahweh is the Alpha and the Omega, the beginning and the end.

Amen. Come, Lord Jesus. The grace of the Lord Jesus be with His people.

Introduction –
They Call Me Potato Chip

I'm not crazy in the purest sense of the word. So far, I haven't shown up at the grocery store in a ball gown and tiara, or done anything else particularly inappropriate ...yet. However, I do get a kick out of catching folks off guard and making them smile, so I have been known to say and do some goofy things or wear some silly outfits. My favorite tools are sarcasm and the term *groovy*. When I say, "Have a groovy day," I hope someone will smile with me.

"You own everything that happened to you. Tell your stories. If people wanted you to write warmly about them, they should have behaved better." -- Anne Lamott

You may have bought this first book of mine out of sheer curiosity because you wonder what I wrote about you (insert mischievous giggle). You may be relieved (or maybe disappointed) to know that I have been somewhat discreet with my stories for one important reason: my mother, my children, and my grandchildren will be reading this, and I've got an image to maintain, for goodness sake. I want to be candid, but will forego any gratuitous violence. Some stories will be saved for telling on another day.

Thank you for coming along on this portion of my journey. Sharing my personal epic drama has been on my heart for several years. It seems a shame to let all that pain go to waste when it could be used to help someone else avoid a few of the pitfalls on their paths. It is no small thing to expose my troubling weaknesses and catastrophic failures and to have them evaluated and picked apart by whoever reads this, but it is worth that risk if sharing these stories can help those who might need assistance while navigating through their own rough and stormy seas.

No one goes through this life without having some tough times. I hope that you will read my stories with all their tears and triumphs, and realize that you're not alone. You'll probably come away with thoughts like this: *If this crazy lady can move past these assorted obstacles to find hope and joy, then I surely can, too.*

It's true. You can.

I believe that the world is hungry – no, starving – for the joy of the Lord. In spite of all that has happened, I have the joy of the Lord and it is truly my strength.

It is my hope that folks from all walks of life will find something useful in my stories. I lived through these moments (some of them were super-long moments) and found strength to overcome a numerous array of adversities by the power of my relationship with Jesus. I expect that those who don't believe as I do might still find some redeeming qualities in these stories. You may be a church-in-your-rocking-chair kind of person, or you may have completely given up on those who are religious and their institutions. You may be at the church building every time the doors are open or you may only come for Easter and Christmas services. Whatever the case, it is my desire for these stories to inspire and encourage you.

Nonetheless, I lay it all out for you to judge for yourself.

And so it was with me, brothers and sisters. When I came to you, I did not come with eloquence or human wisdom as I proclaimed to you the testimony about God. For I resolved to know nothing while I was with you except Jesus Christ and him crucified. I came to you in weakness with great fear and trembling. My message and my preaching were not with wise and persuasive words, but with a demonstration of the Spirit's power, so that your faith might not rest on human wisdom, but on God's power. -- 1 Corinthians 2:1-5

You may read things in here that you don't agree with. That's fair enough. I hope you'll handle it like you would eat a juicy slice of cold watermelon on a hot summer afternoon. Enjoy the good stuff and spit out the seeds.

Who in the world is Potato Chip?
A nickname is bestowed in many ways. Mine came from a silly summer camp song, but we were not children; we were

lively, laughing adult women attending a retreat. It was skit night, and I decided to ham it up on this song with exaggerated body motions and a boisterous attitude. I know, go figure! I'm usually so very shy, quiet and reserved.

Clap to the rhythm (the crowd echoes).
Potato chip, potato chip (Potato chip, potato chip)
I like 'em crunchy, crunchy! (I like 'em crunchy, crunchy!)
And I love Jesus (And I love Jesus)
A bunchy, bunchy! (a bunchy, bunchy!)
Exponentially exaggerate the clapping to extend arms wide on each clap when saying "bunchy, bunchy."

There are a few other verses, but you get the idea.

We didn't sing the song at just one gathering. We met a couple of times a year at this camp, and the song has become an anthem over the years. I attempt to let the memory of it fade away, but it is resurrected each time. "Potato Chip, come sing your song!" And, of course, I give the crowd what they want. It's who I am and what I do, for goodness sake.

In early November 2012, I went to my mailbox, and there was an envelope addressed to *Potato Chip*. How fun is that?! What must the mail carrier have thought? Inside was a card. The gist of the contents was:
A small group of folks gathered over their beloved coffee and discussed life. There were challenging chasms to be spanned and demanding lessons to be learned as they each tried to follow in the Master's footsteps. With laughter and

tears, they showed love to one another as they extended grace for that moment and then granted each other courage. When their mugs were empty, their spirits were full, and they felt energized for the rest of their journey.

We are all working our way through something and are in need of some love, grace, and courage – man or woman, young or old. Sadly, I find myself withholding that from others, but I sure want a big bundle of it for myself.

By exposing who I have been, who I now am and who I want to be, I hope it's readily apparent that the transformation is not my own doing, but the awesome power of the Holy Spirit, doing what He promised He'd do. I can't even fathom *all that is possible* in a Spirit-filled life, but it's exciting to watch what I've seen so far.

As you read through these pages, you'll see these three gifts – love, grace, and courage - threaded through each story with some hope and joy thrown in whenever possible. We're all in this together, and we're not getting out of here alive, so let's use the good 'ol buddy system and help each other over and through the rough patches as we take on this adventure called *life*.

Today, look for someone who needs love, grace, and courage, then give them a bunchy, bunchy! Please, tell them that *Potato Chip* sent you.

I Was Born at a Very Young Age

I have known what it was to have plenty and also what it was to be in need. There is a fear factor as I prepare to share a few of the things that life has given me the *opportunity to experience* (to put it nicely). Please don't think that I lead this charmed, fairy-tale existence and feel it my civic and Christian duty to arrogantly advise you to *hang in there*, no matter how tough life is right now. Oh, no. It isn't like that at all.

The truth is that my life has had some pretty rough patches of road, most of it as a result of my own sparkling stupidity. To my credit, I didn't just wallow in the mistakes, but rather kept putting one foot in front of the other in faith; sometimes crawling, usually crying, and eventually trusting that my God was larger than the giant, huge, very large mountain in front of me. Trusting not in what I could see, but in Who I knew was there.

These next few pages hold a condensed version of the Life of Carrie, highlighting the *opportunities* so far. Some of these *opportunities* will be found, in greater detail, further back in this book.

My momma and daddy told me that I was dearly loved before my first breath was drawn. As childhoods go, I've come to appreciate that mine was pretty spectacular, no doubt, in part because we didn't have to wear a bunch of protective gear to ride our bikes. Come to think of it, that might explain a few things. Maybe I landed on my noggin one too many times.

I grew up on a West Texas farm, surrounded by copious quantities of love and laughter from our large family and close friends. We were social animals. The things I got to do as a kid weren't safe, but life sure was exciting. One of my favorite stunts was to climb up in the grain bin of our towering John Deere combine and see how far I could inch out on the auger spout. I was never as brave as my younger brother, but my talk was big. Go figure.

I was taught to drive a Case tractor and a Chevy pickup when I was in first grade. The great outdoors was filled with adventure and dirt, so I had a blast! Of course, being native Texans, my brother and I were taught to ride a horse, shoot a gun, and watch for snakes. I appreciate that my parents showed my brother, Cory, and me the value of hard work. We had chores inside and outside the house. We both know how to operate the business end of a hoe, an irrigation tube, a washing machine and a spatula.

The older I get, the more thankful I am for their training. It never occurred to me that I was less capable just because I was a girl. We each found out what we enjoyed most and what we did best. That's what growing up is all about: figuring out how to be an adult. I did have some crazy mad cooking skills and could mix up a mean batch of brownies from the time I was in elementary school, thanks to my momma, who is an excellent cook. I also had a serious love of swimming, so I ironed my dad's shirts and just about anything I could get my hands on to earn enough nickels to pay the admission fee for the neighborhood pool during the summer months.

I can't recall a time that I felt unloved or unwanted. Humbly, I realize what a precious gift that is. My heart aches when I hear others tell of childhoods that were filled with abuse, indifference, and fear. I've come to realize what it took for my parents to protect us and to make sure that my brother and I knew we were loved and safe.

My magical childhood was interrupted by my parents' divorce when I was fourteen. I met my knight in shining armor, aka Steve, a few months later and married when I was sixteen. I had our first baby when I was eighteen and our fourth one when I was twenty-two.

(I know. I know. If you do the math on that, you'll find that I was forty when our last child graduated high school. Most folks thought we were nuts to have so many kids so close together. We were, but when I was forty, and the house was empty because the last child was in college, it started to make sense that maybe it wasn't such a bad idea, after all. Fortunately, memory fades with age, and I don't remember all the sleepless nights. I'm not talking about when they were all babies, either. I'm remembering when they were all teenagers. Teenagers teach their parents how to pray and trust, which comes in handy because as those precious teens become adults, start careers, get married, have babies and such, we appreciate praying without ceasing. Can I get an *Amen*?)

When I was nineteen and Steve was twenty-four, a benign tumor was discovered on his jugular vein, which required surgery and a month-long hospital stay. Three years later, we wound up having to file bankruptcy on our farming operation during pregnancy number four. Immediately after birthing sweet number four, I had to have an emergency hysterectomy.

My mom and step-dad kept the older three kiddos for six weeks so I could just care for my newborn and myself. The little darlings would come home for the weekends when Steve was not working, bringing a great deal of noise, energy and motion with them. Just imagine! The baby was not impressed, at all. Shannel would look at me as if to ask, "Who are these people and why are they so loud? When are they leaving?" Needless to say, she wasn't thrilled when they came home to stay after my six week recovery time was complete.

As if I were prolonging my childhood, I waited until the age of twenty-five to have my tonsils out and until I was twenty-eight to get the chicken pox. Shannel innocently brought the chicken pox home from a birthday party and promptly shared them with all of our little family, except Steve, who had the good sense to have childhood illnesses as a child.

Steve and I started a cell phone and satellite TV business in 1996, working together to build it to nine stores and about forty employees over a twelve-year period. We made some poor business decisions and, rather than file bankruptcy again, we chose to pay off the mountain of corporate debt because we felt that it was the right thing to do. The amount was large enough that we put together a twenty-year plan to pay it off. It took only about six years, thanks to hard work, sacrifice, and blessings too numerous to count.

Our kids have brought us lots of love, much laughter and many excuses to pray. They have: been on the Honor Roll and the Dean's List, been suspended from school, been in trouble with the law, used and abused drugs and alcohol, had wrecks, been in the ER, had a baby with a wedding, had a baby without a wedding, graduated college and been to war.

They say that being a parent isn't for sissies. How true that is! When recalling the events of our kids' teen years, I'm thankful that they all survived. It was not a forgone conclusion that they would all grow up. Sometimes, I catch myself complaining about how far away Ashley and her family live, and then I remember that some of my family and friends visit their beloved children's graves. God, bless those parents. I'm ill-equipped to say anything but "I love you, and I will always remember your cherished child."

We've put a wedding on a credit card, and we've paid cash for a wedding. We've experienced living from paycheck to paycheck with no room for error and no savings account. Thankfully, now we have some savings and are not completely upended when the washer breaks or the car needs new tires.

It hasn't been easy. The phone ringing was either a persistent, ill-tempered bill collector, the alarm company with news of a break-in at one of our nine B Wireless stores or one of our children with concerning news. Maybe that's why I got out of the telecom industry - bad memories of ringing telephones.

We moved my mother-in-law in with us for a couple of years, when she was ill and no longer needed to live alone. I also cared for my dad and my Granny at the ends of their lives. Those experiences are like none other and are hard to describe because of the heartbreak and the fascinating beauty of these moments.

Sometimes, I handled the challenges with grace, which is fabulous. But often, I was worried and faithless. Thankfully, there was always someone to encourage me or to set me straight. I'm forever grateful for those who challenged me to be strong and courageous and to never give up.

I figure that we're all doing the best we can most of the time. In the inevitable, horrifying instant when it all goes sideways, and we find ourselves sliding off the road and into a ditch, we don't give up and just sit there. We strive to be strong and courageous, whatever our circumstances, and find our way back up to the road. Afterward, we tell the tale of our misadventure which serves as a warning to others to avoid that same trap, if possible. No matter how it's worded, telling that tale is one way to offer each other grace and inspiration to just keep on keeping on.

"Have I not commanded you? Be strong and courageous. Do not be afraid; do not be discouraged, for the LORD your God will be with you wherever you go." -- Joshua 1:9

The Driver of
That Baby Blue Pickup is Mine

In Littlefield, Texas, in November of 1978, dragging Main Street was a cool thing to do. If you never got to drag Main, it involves lots of fuel, lots of honking and lots of laughter. On any given Friday or Saturday night, you'd pile some friends into the car you borrowed from your parents and head to the center of town.

Main Street in Littlefield was really Phelps Avenue, a two-way street that ran from the County Courthouse to the block before the train depot. We would drive south to the courthouse, make a right-hand turn and wind through a parking lot, then head back north. At the intersection before the train depot, we'd make a right turn and go to Nelson's Hardware, turn around and do it all over again...and again, and again, and again...until curfew. Every teenager in town was doing the same thing, so there was bumper-to-bumper traffic. If the weather was warm, the windows were down and the music was blaring. If the weather was cold, the heater was on high, the windows were down, and the music was blaring. It's difficult to convey just how fun this was!

The Drag was four blocks long, interrupted by four traffic signals. One block to the east of The Drag was a one-way street going south. One block to the west of The Drag was a one-way street going north. If we saw someone we wanted to see again, we just turned at the next intersection and went down the one-way to situate ourselves back on The Drag to pass that person again. That's where my story begins.

On a Saturday night in late November, I was lucky that Kim (a sixteen-year-old licensed driver) was willing to take my best friend, Holly, and me to The Drag with her. We hadn't been there long when we passed a pickup with three cute guys in it. Immediately, I said, "The driver of that baby blue pickup is mine."

I asked Kim to go back around so we could see them again. She made the block via the one-way street, and we were, once again, passing by that pickup full of cute guys. We did that a couple more times and finally got the courage to ask them to pull off The Drag and meet us at the Car Wash, a place to stop and chat. Introductions were made, and I found out that the man of my dreams was named Steve. I made sure the cute driver of that baby blue pickup had my phone number before we parted company that night. I hoped that he would soon give me a call.

Indeed, Steve called me the next week and asked if I'd like to go "get a coke" the next Friday night. Yippee!

I'm not proud of this next part of the story, but you might as well hear it from me. I was fourteen. He was nineteen. I lied to him and told him I was seventeen. Maybe you've heard Sir Walter Scott's quote, "Oh, what a tangled web we weave, when first we practice to deceive." Yeah, well, I'm afraid I chose to keep spinning that web because my parents would have never let me date a guy that old, so I told them he was seventeen. Judge me as you will. I know it was wrong, *but he was so cute*! It was a couple of months before I told him that I was only fourteen. He says that by then it was too late, he was in love. It was over a year before I confessed to my parents and by then, they had gotten used to him being around, but they were not amused, in the least, with my lies.

As I've already mentioned, my parents were divorced. Had they been together and presented a united front, I'm all but certain that Steve and I would not have dated at that or any other time. I'm not saying the end justifies the means, I'm just telling you what happened.

Steve lived in Levelland, a small town about twenty-five miles away, which was a long distance telephone call to Littlefield back in 1978. For the whippersnappers reading this, before unlimited local and long distance cell phone calls, we had corded phones in our homes (that were attached to the wall), and it cost a fortune to talk to someone who lived in another town. His long-distance phone bill ran about $400 a month. Yes, $400! That's true love, wouldn't you say?

We wrote each other letters a couple of times a week, talked on the phone a few times a week and were together a couple of times each weekend. I thought about him all the time. He says that he thought about me all the time, too (insert adorable school-girl giggle.)

My house was about forty-five minutes from Steve's house. He came to see me most Friday and Saturday nights and some Sunday afternoons. I lived fifteen minutes from our small town of Littlefield and about forty-five minutes from the big city of Lubbock. There is no telling how many miles we rode together in the two years that we dated. We made countless trips up and down The Drag in Littlefield with the Eagles, Boston or ELO blasting from the 8-track tape deck. We'd go eat chili cheese hot dogs (which we called Der dogs) and fries at Der Wienerschnitzel, then catch a movie in Lubbock or we'd go to Levelland and make The Drag there. Between the phone bills and gas for his (baby blue) pickup, he invested quite a lot in our relationship.

My cousin, Alvin, took us water skiing a few times. Steve isn't a swimmer, but he loves the water. One day in particular, Steve was out on the inner tube, and Alvin was driving the boat. Alvin asked me, "Do you like this one?" I said, "Yes," but he still gave poor Steve a pretty rough ride out on that tube. No doubt, Alvin was trying to gauge Steve's commitment to either staying alive at all costs or to our relationship. I guess if Steve stuck around after that, he really was a keeper.

We often talked about our future together and about being married. About eighteen months into our relationship, I had an opportunity to go to Europe as a People to People student ambassador. We broke up over some frivolous something or another right before I left for that six weeks, but we wrote each other the whole time. The day after getting home, I called Steve and asked to see him. After that, I began to wonder if we really had to wait until after my high school graduation to get married. My cousin asked me, "Why wait? You could do worse. Steve loves you so much, and he has a good family." I laugh out loud at that memory. She was right. I could have done worse, much worse.

Steve was a farmer, so on one of our Sunday afternoon dates in late July, I was helping him move irrigation pipe on his farm. I asked, "What if we don't wait to get married?" He just stared at me, then asked, "Really?"

There was no formal proposal on bended knee; there were no roses or other elaborately planned events. There were logistics of talking to my parents and my finishing high school in Levelland. Neither was an easy task, but we sure did think outside the box to make it all happen. Where there's a will, there's a way. My mother said that she sent me to Europe to see that there was more to the world than marrying a farmer from Levelland. But, this young gal had seen the world and still wanted the farmer from Levelland.

Planning our wedding was fun, but with my parents freshly divorced, the relationships were not conducive to an entirely joyful event. Don't misunderstand – I was as sure of myself as a sixteen-year-old schoolgirl could be, and I had a streak of determination that helped me make up my mind and move me past the challenges. The ceremony was beautiful with flowers, music, love and some well-dressed attendants. The pretty girls wore gorgeous pink floppy garden hats and the guys were ever-so-handsome in snazzy tuxedos with ruffled pink shirts. I know. It *was* special.

As I visited with close friends and family in the church hallway a few minutes before walking down the aisle, my friend's mom, Norma Kay, gently took me by the shoulders and looked deeply into my eyes as she said, "Honey, give it all you've got."

I vaguely remember others talking to me and offering advice, but Norma Kay's words have stayed with me all these years. Give it all you've got. Sometimes I did and sometimes, I didn't. We had the same growing pains every married couple has as they make two lives into one. When there were those inevitable disagreements through the years, I'd ask myself, "Is this all you've got?" Often, the answer was "No" and I'd go back with a better attitude to resolve the issue. Stubborn? Determined to not fail? Yep. I reckon that worked in my favor.

I wonder, how many folks didn't have any hope that our marriage would survive? I'll always be grateful for those words and for my memory popping them into my brain just when I needed them most through the years. We've been married for more than thirty-five years now, so I guess there's something to making a commitment and remembering to "give it all you've got."

My dear and talented friend, Sharlan Proper, wrote a song, *Give It All You've Got*, based on our marriage story.

Standing at the back of the church, dressed in white,
sixteen years to my name.
My best friend's mom grabbed my shoulders and said,
"Honey, give it all you've got."
I leaned on my dad as the doors opened wide,
I looked for her face in the crowd.
As her eyes met mine, she mouthed this refrain,
"Honey, give it all you've got!"

Chorus:
Give it all you've got, then give it all again.
That's how you give it all you've got for your life-long love.

Lying on my back in the bed I had made,
I heard the door slam below.
He stomped to the fields; I heard those old words,
"Honey, give it all you've got!"
I sat on the porch as the dust cloud arrived.
He looked at me with a doubt.
I took him inside and swallowed my pride.
"I'm not giving all I've got."

Standing at the back of a crowd, near the tree,
grinning from ear to ear.
The kids on their knees, the grandkids in tow;
what a life of joy we share!

The problems seem small, the happiness great,
oh what a life we live!
The cameras all click, the crowd scatters wild.
I'm glad we're giving all we've got.[1]

As the third verse of this song suggests, the relationship that my Pransome Hince and I have is pretty extraordinary these days (surely, you watched Hee Haw when you were a child). But please, don't think for one instant that it *just happened*, or we were *lucky*. We are not especially well-paired, nor are we soul mates. We worked at our relationship. We worked hard.

We've had many brushes with the death of our marriage, but we kept our covenant vows to one another and chose to forgive, overlook and persevere. Many times we made a conscious choice to stay when we wanted to leave or to hold our tongue when we wanted to spew hateful, hurtful words. I would tell myself, "I love Steve more than I hate _____."

Sometimes I filled in the blank with "how he leaves his clothes on the floor" or "how he insists on needing milk and Nestle Quik on hand at all times". When I could do that, I could see past the present yuckiness and see hope for our future. If I gave in to all the little annoyances, or if he did, our marriage couldn't recover.

(We did have one teeny, tiny, little bitty addition to our wedding vows that may have played a teeny, tiny, little bitty

---

[1] *Give It All You've Got*, by Sharlan Proper, from the album, *Simple Words*

22

part in keeping us together. We knew that whoever left would have to take all four kids. Neither of us had that kind of courage or wanted to leave that badly. Bahahahaha!)

Maybe this will make sense: although I always love Steve, I've had days that I didn't like him. He's felt the same about me, to be sure. Fortunately, there have been many more days that we've been crazy in love with each other, which has sure helped us in honoring our covenant with one another.

Ok, so *honoring our covenant with each other* sounds lovely, doesn't it? Marriage is so much more than keeping a promise to love, honor and cherish. It's truly intertwining my very being with my husband; making every part of *me* become *us* so that there is no way to see where one starts and the other ends.

The two will become one flesh. Let's see...where have I read that? (*Genesis 2:24*)

Commitment is hard work that has been well-worth the effort. There was a specific occasion when I knew the decision to persevere in our marriage was the best decision. Our first two grandbabies were born within four days of one another. I would watch Steve love on those babies, and it thrilled me to have him experience that joy as much as if I had been holding the precious baby myself. I knew then that if we had not stayed together, I'd have been jealous to have him hold them. True love shows itself when we want more for that other person than we want for ourselves. My heart still smiles when I remember that moment. It's one of my favorite memories.

These are the types of moments that take my breath away and bring tears to my eyes, those moments of pure love. It's not white-hot passion, but smoldering selflessness, which is infinitely better. *That's* what love looks like, folks. It's when one person looks out for the best interest of another. I can't imagine anything better.

So, for all the bookmakers from that fateful night in December of 1980, I hope you bet on the right pony, because if I had it to do all over again, I'd do it *all over again.*

No More Sleeping in on Sundays

Steve wasn't so interested in going to church and I didn't want to go alone, so I didn't. We slept in on Sunday mornings.

I was a young woman, neither mature in my faith nor bold in my convictions. I remember hoping that Steve would someday decide to think about Jesus and salvation, but I didn't know how to talk to him about it, except to ask at Easter and Christmas if he'd go to church with me. I didn't want to be annoying to the point that he just had no interest, so I did the safe thing. Nothing.

We had our first two babies not quite thirteen months apart, born in October of 1982 and 1983. One night in late December of '83, we were in our bedroom, getting ready for bed. I can still see this moment so clearly in my mind's eye. Maybe Steve was thinking about his New Years' resolutions as he said, "I want the kids to be raised in the church."

I stopped dead in my tracks. My heart started beating faster as I cautiously asked him, "Am I going with you or are you going with me?"

We were raised in different churches, so this was a definite fork in the road for us. He said, "I'll go with you." I said, "Ok."

That was it; the whole life-altering conversation. Such eloquence, wouldn't you agree?

We lived in Levelland and went to the church on Cactus Drive the first Sunday in January 1984. This started a new way of life for our family. We didn't have to wonder what we were going to be doing every Sunday morning for the rest of our lives. That decision had been made. It was one of our big rocks. (We'll chat more about that big rock later.)

There's a great deal of power in making a decision once and living with it, rather than revisiting it over and over again, questioning if it was the right decision. It's exhausting and a waste of time.

By the second week of February, (yes, six weeks later) Steve had been diagnosed with a tumor on his jugular vein. He had started losing the hearing in his right ear the previous year, so his doctor ordered a CT scan, which revealed nothing, so the doctor attributed it to Steve's having been on a tractor most of his life and listening to loud music. Then in January of 1984 (yes, the very month we started attending worship services), Steve noticed fluid in his right ear.

His doctor sent him to a specialist in Lubbock who admitted him to Methodist Hospital and began running various tests. At the end of the day, as Steve was lying in his hospital bed after an arteriogram, the doctor came in with the results. A benign glomus tumor had grown on his jugular vein just as the blood vessel made a crook right by his ear. As the tumor grew, it ate through those bones in his middle ear, the stirrup, hammer, and anvil, leaving him with no hearing in that ear.

Surgery was required, so he was given four options, one of which was a neurosurgeon in Lubbock who told us that he *thought he could get it all.* Steve marked him off the list first. After weighing his remaining three options, Steve chose to go to Dr. Gardner in Memphis TN, who had pioneered this particular surgery with two of his colleagues. (This was ultimately the very best choice for him, as he received amazing care from those doctors and the incredible medical team at Baptist Memorial Hospital. I'd call it a success, as it's been over thirty years, and our kids had a healthy daddy to raise them.)

He had several weeks of radiation treatments and countless doctor visits to prepare him for the best outcome of the surgery that was planned for late in May. Since he had to go for radiation four times a week for six weeks, a couple of the teenaged girls from church came on those days to help me by washing bottles, folding laundry and playing with Ashley and Josh.

Our new church family was very attentive, supportive and prayerful for him. They wrapped their arms around him and showed him how *John 13:34-35* looked in action. They came to our home to hug us and pray with us. They brought delicious food. They took the time to go out and buy cards, write sweet notes of encouragement and mail them to him. They showed Steve what Jesus' love felt like.

One Sunday in April, without a word to me, Steve got up at the close of the sermon, during the invitation song and headed to the front of the sanctuary. He was baptized that day, as I sat there alone in the pew, stunned. Perhaps my character won him over, but more likely, it just didn't chase him away. No doubt, the surgery he was facing in May and his thoughts of survival and eternity played a larger role. Sometimes, it just helps if we don't do any harm. Right?

Upon returning home from a month in the hospital, he was quite weak and had lost thirty pounds. (Heckuva way to do it!) Summertime was in full-swing, so we had the evaporative cooler running, but he was on the sofa, covered with a couple of thick blankets because he was so cold. During those difficult days, a well-meaning lady said, "It'll just take some time."

I remember wanting to scream, "Do you have any idea what a day looks like for me?" I had a very sick husband, a twenty-month-old and an eight-month-old. Time crawled by ever so slowly. Yes, in time everything was better, but I learned a valuable lesson: folks who are hurting need hope and encouragement for *that moment*, not platitudes and a pat on the head.

Here's where conviction comes in and grabs me by my lapels: How many times do I look on those who are hurting, hungry or cold and just wish them well, but never lift a finger to serve them? Hmmm...

What good is it, my brothers and sisters, if someone claims to have faith but has no deeds? Can such faith save them? Suppose a brother or a sister is without clothes and daily food. If one of you says to them, "Go in peace; keep warm and well fed," but does nothing about their physical needs, what good is it? -- James 2:14-16

Telling you this part of my story reminds me that the Almighty really is omnipotent, omniscient and omnipresent. He loves us enough to pursue us, tapping us on the shoulder, reminding us that He can help, if we'll let Him.

Because of these Jesus followers' great love for our little family, we worshiped and shared our lives with them until we moved to Lubbock ten years later. They helped both of us learn to teach Bible classes. These men and women showed us the wonders of potluck meals, rowdy game nights and a couple of unruly scavenger hunts. They loved us as we were when we got there, but then they loved us enough to cultivate our little seedling faith.

I shudder to remember what I gave them to work with. I was loud and mouthy, and figured that everyone was entitled to my opinion on a variety of topics, whether I was an expert on the subject or not. I would do or say just about anything. You probably wouldn't have liked me back then. Really, I'm not sure why everyone didn't get fed up with me to the point that they claimed they never even knew me. Seriously, I was a hot mess! Fortunately, some could see the little glimmer of potential within me. I'm so thankful for the grace they showered on to me.

Even now, when we visit there, they wrap their arms around us as if to say, "Welcome home." I've often said that this is a glimpse of what Heaven will be like. I can get excited about hugs and jubilation as we meet our Lord face-to-face. I don't want to miss that!

Get Real

I beg you – please don't confuse God with the church and church-going folks. They are not the same thing, though I wish they were.

I have been told that some folks stay home from the worship assembly because they feel that the pews are filled with hypocrites, or they feel that they are too big a sinner for the Lamb of God to want them, or they are just too tired or mad, or they aren't ready to admit their sin because there's plenty of time. More and more, I wonder if it's because *church* has become a joyless, monotonous ritual where no worship or praise is lifted high from the pew packers. I understand all of these excuses.

When we see good church folks looking down their noses at us on Sunday, then we see them holler and cuss to their employees and cheat their customers Monday through Friday, then get drunk on Saturday, it is a little hard to picture sitting in the pew with them.

When we look in the mirror and are disgusted with the pitiful, weak person staring back at us, it's hard to imagine that The King could want us. How could someone so filthy sit in a pew and dare hope that the righteous Redeemer would care?

I get it. I can't explain it all away because I've felt all these same things. And, while it is always tempting, I can't let myself get caught up in other folks' bad behavior. I am only accountable for myself. There are many interpretations of scripture, but at the end of the day, I have to answer this question: "If I died right now, would I feel sure of my salvation, based on what the scriptures say?"

Heaven is real. Hell is real. God is real. Satan is real. There is a wide road and a narrow road. I can let this scare me or I can let it inspire me. I choose the latter.

As we were having babies and building our own clan, we became more involved with our church family. We had hectic lives with a bunch of little ones running around the house and yard.

In fact, many times, we had little ones bringing the yard in the house. When the kids are all pre-school age, they loved playing in the water (and mud). We'd wake up in the morning and realize either the front yard or the backyard was flooded. The little darlings were just the right height to turn on the outdoor water faucets so they could play in the glorious wetness, so they did. They had such fun.

When Josh was almost three, he came walking into the kitchen with the garden hose spewing water. *Into the kitchen*! After that, Steve took the faucet handles off. We used a pair of pliers to operate the faucets until the littles got to be not-so-littles. Ahhh, the kiddos - they kept us on our toes.

Because I wanted to be a great mommy, I tried to live a *real* life. I didn't want to be one of those moms who yelled and screamed at my family (those I love most on this planet) as they had hurriedly wolfed down breakfast and gotten dressed on Sunday morning, then arrived at the church building with a pasted-on smile and forced oh-so-kind words for everyone else. I made a grand effort to be the same person at home that I was away from home.

I'm not sure how successful I was, but hopefully, the effort paid off a little bit. I'm afraid that I did do some yelling...but it wasn't on Sunday mornings. Maybe it was as we tried to be on time to catch the school bus or maybe at bedtime. Or, when they flooded the yard. Yikes!

Part of being a *real* person included not telling little lies. When someone called on the phone, I never lied about being busy nor did I ask Steve to tell the caller I wasn't home when I was. I didn't roll my eyes in exasperation and then fake a syrupy sweet voice as I took the call. (You know the tone of voice I'm talking about.)

I didn't gossip. My momma told me that if my friends gossiped about their other friends when they were with me, then they were gossiping about me when they were with their other friends. (Aren't mommas so smart?!) None of that has ever played well with me. It's easy to get caught up in conversation, thinking that we're just informing others of a situation. But, it degrades quickly, and we find ourselves knowing things that are none of our business.

Sometimes, gossip is disguised innocently enough, and we tell a secret so that "everyone can be praying about it." That's satan and some more of his lies! (satan doesn't deserve a capital S because I refuse to give him that much power.) The times that my feelings were hurt the most were when close friends betrayed a confidence by starting off a conversation with others by saying, "We need to be praying for the Blairs..."

"...busybodies who talk nonsense, saying things they ought not to." -- 1 Timothy 5:13

There's a lot to be said for minding our own business, isn't there?

Proverbs has several verses on gossip:
A gossip betrays a confidence – 11:13a
A perverse person stirs up conflict, and a gossip separates close friends. – 16:28
A gossip betrays a confidence; so avoid anyone who talks too much. – 20:19
Without wood a fire goes out; without a gossip, a quarrel dies down. – 26:20

I've been in situations where someone started talking about someone who was not there, gossiping, and I've said, "I'd rather not talk about her/him if she/he isn't here." It shocks them at first, but word gets around, and folks don't ask me back over for coffee because I'm just no dadgum fun if I won't participate.

Fair enough.

Becoming *real* is not letting the world tell you who you should be so that you feel the need to exaggerate or lie to fit someone else's expectations. It's about being who you were created to be. Sometimes, that can be messy. I have an increasingly poor memory, so I've learned that it's just easier to tell the truth so I only have to remember *one story*. I've squirmed more than once as I've had to come clean and speak the truth in uncomfortable circumstances. It is said that the hardest conversations are the most important ones.

I'm guilty of proudly wearing my marriage and my motherhood like a badge of honor. In doing that, my arrogance had stopped conversations before they even started. Celebrating anniversaries and Mother's Day isn't the problem, my prideful attitude is. I'm not defined by anything except my heart for others.

I have a new friend who tells me what she thinks I want to hear. I remember doing the same thing around those I had just met or that I wanted to impress. At some point in my long and winding road toward maturing, I realized that if I was so embarrassed by my true self, then maybe it was time to make some changes.

We all come to that point, don't we? I'd rather show the world that I've got my life all together, but reality is that I don't. I make a zig when I should have made a zag. I say things that hurt others. Sometimes, I get caught up in the moment, and I find myself swept along on the tide, winding up in situations that I'd rather have avoided.

Oopsie! There has been a bunchy, bunchy of those.

The book of *Ecclesiastes* tells us that there is nothing new. From generation to generation, things are now as they have always been. Humankind behaves as we have always behaved.

Sigh.

I go to worship assembly on Sunday morning with my life in order. When someone asks, "How are you today?" I reply, "Fine."

Because I am, right? Right. I am perfect. My marriage is perfect. My children are perfect. My job is perfect. My bank account is perfect. My past is perfect.

Why aren't we *real*? We could reply, "I'm a sinner. I said (or did) some things I shouldn't have this last week." When we look like we have it all together, others don't want to expose their own weakness and pain. I have noticed in recent years that more churches are saying things like "There are no perfect people here." That is freeing! I can be *real*.

Unfortunately, the church can have a reputation for shooting the wounded. There are times and places for Jesus' followers to discern and offer instruction. Of course, when some soul is in danger, we could *lovingly* instruct with scripture. Oh, how I wish that were always the case.

Judging is harsh and unloving. When I'm caught in a sin, I get defensive, so that even loving correction and instruction can feel like I just got swats from the principal. The test comes when I must ask myself if I would rather have been left alone to die or if I would want to have my sin exposed so restoration could begin.

A couple of years ago, I was on staff at a ladies spiritual renewal weekend where about a dozen of us share our testimonies. We tell about our personal trials and sins, then we share how the power of the Cross, the love of our Savior, and the guidance of The Spirit, led us out of that period of darkness into hope and peace.

One sweet young lady sat beside me, and her eyes welled up with tears. She said, "I'm concerned about telling my story. I'm afraid of what you'll think of me afterward." I held her and assured her that nothing she could ever say or do would make me not love her. She said, "I know that you'll love me, but I don't think you'll like me after you hear it." I held her close and let her know that wasn't even possible. And I meant it.

Psalm 32 starts - *Blessed is the one whose transgressions are forgiven, whose sins are covered. Blessed is the one whose sin the* LORD *does not count against them and in whose spirit is no deceit.*

God bless her for her precious heart. She was willing to *be real* to help others see the power that God can and *will* wield in our lives if we ask Him and then *let* Him.

It's not fun. Sin is always ugly, and it always separates us from the Holy One. We can't dress it up or make it palatable. We just have to confess it, ask forgiveness and move on down the road. Thankfully, that is always an option with God.

If we confess our sins, He is faithful and just and will forgive us our sins and purify us from all unrighteousness. --1 John 1:9

That's some more good news, isn't it! Because of His great love for us, we can be redeemed, healed and restored.

So, let's be *real* with each other when we meet at the grocery store or in the church pew. I am a sinner. I struggle with pride, food, selfishness and a smart-aleck mouth. I am not perfect, and my life isn't perfect, but I am redeemed. I am healed. I am restored.

I am real.

Hello, My Name is Carrie, and I'm a Control Freak

I love being in control. I like my To Do lists and my datebook so I can plan for tomorrow, next week, next month and next year. I rarely start a day with nothing on my To Do list. It's not just about being busy because there is always something to clean, cook or repair. It's about having a plan and *feeling secure* about my plan - *relying* on my list.

Feeling secure about my plan? *Relying* on my To Do list? *Relying* on my datebook? Really?

A list isn't evil nor is a datebook evil, just like money isn't evil. How I use these tools can be the problem. Anything that I allow to come between God and me is a problem. It can be my To Do lists. It can be my family. It can be my job. It can be my favorite television show. It can be Facebook. It can be chocolate.

One of my struggles is control. Who is in control? Me or God?

My being in control of anything is merely an illusion because I can't control my hair, much less my life!

As a teenager, I thought I had all the answers. What a gift to be sixteen years old and know everything! Every. Thing. By the time I was thirty, it was apparent that I didn't really know so much and by the time I had teenagers, I was calling my mom and dad to apologize for my own behavior as a teen. I was paying for my raising! We think, "I'm an adult now. I've got it all figured out." News flash - we don't! Not even close. I *still* don't have it all figured out, and I'm fifty-something years old.

But, Someone who loves me very much absolutely does have it figured out.

For I know the plans I have for you, declares the Lord, plans to prosper you and not to harm you, plans to give you hope and a future. -- Jeremiah 29:11

Our buddy, Wayne Newman once told me, "Two people cannot create a soul. It doesn't matter if they are married or in the back seat of a Chevy, only God can create an eternal being."

Obviously, those words have stayed with me. I've shared them with anyone that might need to hear them. They are pure truth. God didn't make a mistake. A couple of lusty young adults might have made a poor choice, but an innocent baby is an eternal being and is no accident. Ever.

If you were that lusty young adult or that innocent baby, The King of Kings loves you.

For you created my inmost being; you knit me together in my mother's womb. I praise you because I am fearfully and wonderfully made; your works are wonderful, I know that full well. My frame was not hidden from you when I was made in the secret place when I was woven together in the depths of the earth. Your eyes saw my unformed body; all the days ordained for me were written in your book before one of them came to be. -- Psalm 139:13-16

And then there's *Jeremiah 1:5*
Before I formed you in the womb, I knew you.

Read those verses again if you have to. We were no surprise to Abba. No baby is a surprise to The Father. He has known us since before He took the time to knit us together in our mother's womb! We have a purpose.

Without a doubt in my mind, I can confidently say that we each have a purpose. There is a big picture, a plan. Imagine a puzzle is spread out on the table. It doesn't matter if it is an 8-piece puzzle or one of those with thousands of pieces; each piece matters, doesn't it? If a piece is missing, then the picture just isn't all that it could be. We can't discount our piece in the big picture.

I wish I could stand here and tell you about my perfect children who have never back-talked me, and how my beloved husband and I have never uttered a cross word to one another, and that I never gave my sweet mother a moment's worry, or that I've never missed a single loan payment, but I can't. I've had hard times physically, emotionally, spiritually and financially. Our family faced illness, death, bankruptcy, drugs, alcohol and unplanned pregnancy. In the toughest times, wise people advised me to *look outside myself and help someone else.*

What? I was having a grand time at my very own pity party, complete with balloons, streamers, chocolate cake and fruit punch. (How embarrassing.)

Maybe *I* was the answer to someone else's prayer?

The greatest commandment asks us to love, so if we are hard-wired to do anything, it is to love. One of the ways we express that love is in serving others: our family, our friends, our neighbors.

When I look outside my own need and search for those to love and to serve, it's like I found the golden key to discovering my purpose. One thing leads to another - as I began to love and serve, I found joy and peace. After that, I found myself full of hope. It became more and more fun to unwrap one gift and find that there was another one waiting. I never get tired of being amazed by God's goodness toward me.

Each new day is filled with its own adventures and surprises. When I wake up and sincerely seek to fulfill my purpose, it is wondrously revealed. When I question my purpose in life, it is usually at a point when my focus becomes disoriented and I am wandering aimlessly, asking only to satisfy myself.

In those tough times, I ask, "Do I have enough faith?" "Is there something wrong with me?" "Will this ever be over?" Experience tells me that it will all work out for the best, and my family will be okay, but the bumpy road isn't so much fun. It rattles my teeth and messes up my hair.

For my personal sanity, it's best for me to sit in sacred quiet every day; to breathe deeply and let go of the *hurry up*. This takes a good bit of effort on my part. I turn off the TV and realize that there is so much *noise* all around me. How in the world can I expect to hear that still, small voice if there is nothing but cacophony all day, every day? I sit. I listen to the quietness. I try to fill myself with peace and feel a calmness wash over me.

I cannot run on "empty", so either I sputter to a stop or take the time to fill my hypothetical tank. I've done both, and it's more desirable to be refreshed and re-energized. There were times that I mustered the energy to make this happen. Other times, I believe that God slowed me down to the point that rest was the only option available. When I had an illness, there was no choice but to stop. (It's a good thing I'm not stubborn.)

Stuff happens in life. There is an analogy of our lives being a series of valleys and mountains. When things are good, we don't have the need to be on our knees before the Father like we do when things are going badly.

I've had the electricity, gas, and phone turned off because the bill wasn't paid. That is humiliating, let me just say. In deep, dark valleys like that, I tried to glean a lesson from the experience – I might as well make it count for something. When I was on top of the mountain, winning all the sales contests and depositing money in the bank, there wasn't much personal growth happening.

Have you ever been to a cemetery for a funeral and taken the time to walk around, looking at the various headstones? There is a date of birth and a date of death carved into each grave marker. Sometimes, there is a scripture verse or some sentiment that reveals a bit more about the person or, at least, a bit about how their descendants viewed that person. My curiosity is piqued, and I wonder about their lives. I daydream about my grave marker. What do you think about this one? *Here we bury merry Carrie who's hairy was scary.* (I crack myself up!)

Ahem. But, I digress. How does one sum up a *lifetime* in a few words?

Then I get to thinking about that dash between their date of birth and their date of death. You've probably heard this story before, but it bears repeating: Life was lived in that dash. All the hopes, dreams, loves, losses, despair, grief, joy and adventure that any life experiences is held in the dash on a gravestone.

God wants control of my dash because He gave that dash to me. *Control?* Control.

There is the story of a professor of philosophy that stood before his class with some items in front of him. When the class began, he wordlessly picked up a large empty mason jar and proceeded to fill it with rocks about two inches in diameter. He then asked the students if the jar was full. They agreed that it was full.

So the professor then picked up a box of pebbles and poured them into the jar. He shook the jar lightly and watched as the pebbles rolled into the open areas between the rocks. The professor then asked the students again if the jar was full.

The class began to sit up and pay attention, nodding that the jar was full. The professor picked up a box of sand and poured it into the jar. The sand filled the remaining open areas of the jar. "Now," said the professor "is the jar full?"

They chuckled and agreed that it was full this time.

Then the professor poured from a water glass until the jar was, indeed, full.

I hope we all recognize that this jar signifies our lives. The big rocks are the most important things, such as God, our family, and our health. If all else was lost and only those three rocks remained, life would still hold significant meaning and hope. The pebbles are the other things that matter in life, such as friends, church work, career or schooling. The sand and water signify the things that are nice, but not necessary. If we put sand and water into the jar first, there is no room for the rocks or the pebbles. The same can be applied to our lives. If we spend all our time and energy on the small stuff, we will never have room for the things that are truly important. We will have compromised our dash.

We get to choose our big rocks, our most important priorities. The jar can be emptied, and we can make new choices. Our choices will always have consequences, so the sooner we make our wisest final selections, the better.

Here's where that "trial and error" part of life comes in. I'm not proud to tell you that it took me a long while to get my God Rock in the jar. When I finally did that, I realized that He means what He says and that He keeps His promises. He created us, He loves us, and He knows what's best for us.

I hope you'll take some time to consider your jar of rocks. Are you happy with your choices? Do you want to make new choices? Is your Family Rock smaller than your Career Rock? Is your God Rock really just a God Pebble?

You can make any changes today or any day. I love that! It's more beautiful than I imagined. God does His best work when I'm not in His way. I choose to release my controlling death-grip. Groovy? *Groovy.*

Did you know The Bible can be used as an Instruction Book? Who knew? Sure enough, there are instructions that pertain to just about everything, including marriage. He asks me to love, forgive and submit.

Wait. What? Submit?

(Yes. Just hang with me for a few more paragraphs, please. I'm not sure why the word "submit" raises my hackles, but it does. Oh, wait. I do know why - I am a control freak. Oh, yeah. I'm still working to remind myself that I'm not in control; never have been, never will be.)

Submit to one another out of reverence for Christ. Wives, submit to your husbands as to the Lord. Husbands, love your wives, just as Christ loved the church and gave himself up for her to make her holy.
-- Ephesians 5:21, 22, 25

There are a few other valuable instructions to wives and husbands in that chapter, but let's focus on verse 21. How about we love Christ enough to *respect each other*? How about I submit to my husband and make a home for our family? Let my husband figure out how he is going to submit to the Lord and love me as Christ loved the church.

Maybe you're thinking – "But my husband doesn't love me like Christ loves the church!" That is, sadly, sometimes the case. I've looked over the verses many times and I just can't seem to find any translation that has an "if" in those verses. "Submit to your husband *if* he submits to the Lord" or "*If* he loves you as Christ loves the church." Those words are just not in there.

*Disclaimer –If you are in an abusive relationship, that is a whole different issue. I do not condone abuse. Ever. So, please seek those who can help you.

As I confessed earlier, I like being in control. I won't go into *all* that I did wrong, but I will share a few key failures with you. I was a nag. I had a mean, filthy mouth. I didn't fight fair. I was manipulative. As a control freak, I was always right, and I refused to listen to how I might not be right.

However, that's not how it worked out. When I forced my agenda, it failed every single time. Every. Single. Time.

When I treated my husband as if he already was the man God wanted him to be, even the worst plan (in my opinion), was exactly the right plan. When I told him that I trusted him, guess what happened? Over time, he *became* the husband of my dreams. I did not foresee that we'd have the life we now share. I've learned that people live up or down to our expectations. (Please keep in mind that we didn't have a faith-based relationship when we met and married. We've come a long way, baby.)

I hate that I thought I knew best, putting my husband down and expecting him to be someone that he just wasn't. I made it impossible for him to be anything but bitter.

Ouch!

There was a period of time that we were merely going through the motions of being married. Nothing good was happening, and we didn't really like each other. The evil one was having his way in our lives, enticing us to bear the fruits of darkness.

Every single thing annoyed us, both in our home and in our marriage. When we escaped our home and went to our respective workplaces, temptations came from people, power and money for both of us. Personally, I was acting and talking in ways that were not right and that were taking me on a path away from my family. In my gut, I knew I was wrong, but it was easier to ride the tide than to fight for what I knew was right.

(Special note - I made a decision long ago to never cast my husband in a bad light. It was one of the smarter things I did. So as you read this, know that I own my part of our marital problems. He has owned his part and if he wants to write a book and tell you about it, he can, but you won't hear it from me.)

During this time, I was at the church building with my family every time the doors were opened. Because sitting in the pews makes everything alright. Right?

We lived out in the country, and we burned our trash in a 55-gallon barrel, like country folks do. One day, after I lit the trash, a piece of the hot plastic garbage bag dripped on my forearm. I had to peel that fiery glob off my arm. It hurt so badly! I vividly remember thinking "If Hell is worse than this, I want no part of it." Talk about getting the message. Whew! I was convicted to get back on the straight and narrow path. I was not the wife or mother that God had created me to be. *Proverbs 14* tells us that *a wise woman builds her house, but a foolish one tears hers down with her own hands.* I was a foolish woman. My house (marriage) was falling down around me, and it was my own doing.

Sometimes, God has to bring out the big guns to get our attention, doesn't He? That burn was just the bolt of lightning from Heaven that I needed to jar me from my selfish stupor. I never enjoy those times of reckoning, but I am thankful for them. God has tried to get my attention many times over the years. As I get older, it's easier to see, thank goodness. Of course, there have been countless mistakes. Sins. The word "mistakes" sounds better, but the reality is that I am a sinner, and I sin.

I love the lyrics to the last verse of *O, Sacred Head*:
What language shall I borrow to thank thee, dearest friend, for this thy dying sorrow, thy pity without end? O make me thine forever; and should I fainting be, Lord, let me never, never outlive my love for thee.

I fervently pray that I never outlive my love for Him. I'd rather die young than die lost.

It was difficult for me to forgive myself for the sins that led me to repent when my arm was burned. I had confidence that God forgave me because my repentance was heartfelt and pure, but the memories of my failure were a sorrow-filled burden that I would drag around for a few miserable years.

I was attending a class at the Abilene Christian University Bible Teachers Workshop where I saw an image of a rugged caveman with a rope wrapped around a large boulder in such a way that he could drag that big ol' rock everywhere he went. The song playing in the background was a song that I'd never heard, *Just Come In* by Margaret Becker. Some of the first lyrics are:
What do I see you draggin' up here, is that for your atoning? I wish you would just come in. Just leave that right there. Love does not care.[2]

I sat there with tears streaming down my face, my whole body trembling. I was so bone-weary of the guilt and shame of my sins – my personal boulder – and the fear of being

---

[2] *Just Come In*, by Margaret Becker, from the album, Immigrant's Daughter

exposed as a make-believe Christian. Apparently, I had been content to drag that big ol' rock around everywhere I went. Memories of my past actions replayed on a constant loop in my mind. I had been unwilling to give up control of my self-imposed consequences. Surely, I didn't deserve to live a life of peace, I told myself.

My mind was racing as I silently sobbed. No one looked my way, and I felt as though the world was frozen in time. For the first time, I felt that maybe I could forgive myself, but in the next second, that hope would swing back to my old habit of self-condemnation. Did I warrant the mercy of just dropping my boulder at Jesus' feet? It seemed too easy. The battle within me was fierce. Give it up. Keep it. Give it up. Keep it.

On the way home, I bought the cassette tape with that song and played it over and over again. I read the scriptures that reminded me that when Jesus forgives, He remembers the sin no more. Finally, I was able to relinquish control of that big ol' rock to Jesus. Only then, was I able to embrace all the joy and peace that comes with letting God into every part of my life and kicking satan to the curb. Once I *surrendered*, the battle was *won*. I was *FREE*! How ironic is that?

God wants us to trust Him, whatever happens. As I've read *Philippians*, there are a few times Paul mentions the phrase *whatever happens*. The first one is in *1:27 - Whatever happens, conduct yourselves in a manner worthy of the Gospel of Christ.*

Whatever happens? Yes, no matter what happens.

Ok, now here was the part that made me pause; this is the part that scared the dickens out of me. How can I just turn everything over to God? I know He loves me. Sure. I've read the scripture and sang the song about Him being the Potter and me being the clay and Him breaking me and re-making me. That is bound to hurt, and I don't really want to hurt any more than I already do. What if He chooses to do that to me?

Then it hit me. What if He doesn't?

What if He doesn't break me and re-make me? Do I stay just like I am now? Is that a good thing? More often than I like to recall, I've rejected His best for me. It can't be good to reject God's best. Yet, I did.

Sometimes, I still do.

I had to make a conscious decision to let Him unconditionally have my life because I knew that staying the same meant that I wasn't truly His. I'd made a mess of my life, so I figured He wouldn't make it any worse. It dawned on me that living my life with me at the controls meant that I didn't trust Him. Why did I find it so difficult? If I do give myself entirely to Him, is it always going to be easy? Nope.

Are bad things going to happen? Yep.

But, I have to ask myself, is my own personal record any better? When I don't trust Him is life easy? Nope.

Do bad things happen? Yep.

The difference is I am not the Creator of the Universe. He is. I can trust Him, *whatever happens.*

I've read the end of The Book. We win! God is victorious! He is the God of the Universe. He is the Lord of Creation. He has conquered death with the power of the Cross and is infinitely worthy of my trust.

The peace that comes from that realization is more soothing to my soul than savoring a white chocolate Lindor truffle while hiding in my dark pantry. And folks, let me just tell you, that's saying something pretty spectacular.

There is Something in the Water

I told you the part of my story where I surrendered my will to live and breathe in His will.
Check.

I shared with you the song that touched something inside me and triggered a flood of emotions and a life-changing decision.
Check.

Carrying around the guilt and shame had taken the place of my joy and my hope. Once I surrendered, I could see it all so clearly.

For me, it took a concentrated period of time of being honest with myself and spending time with Jesus; focusing on His sacrifice and all that it meant. When it hit me that He'd already forgiven me, that He still loved me and that I was *disrespecting His gift*, I was able to drop that boulder at His feet, thank Him and walk away. Old habits are hard to break, so when the old feelings started creeping back in,

I'd remind myself that it was over, and I'd picture that big ol' rock at Jesus' feet.

Then, I learned to live like I'd been forgiven. I spent time in His Word and planted His words in my heart. I began to love others because I was finally able to love myself. I was able to forgive others because I'd been forgiven. I started making an effort to see people the way Jesus sees them.

(I wish I was a quick learner, but I'm not. The process did drag just a little bit when I would get caught up in me, me, me. I'm sure you wouldn't have that problem. Right? My life has been a bunch of baby steps to get from point A to point B and so on. I can hope to re-read these words in a few years and think "Oh, dear. You have certainly matured since then.")

What did it look like when I say I began to live like I'd been forgiven? First of all, I came out of the oppressive dungeon and into the glorious daylight where there was joy and laughter. There was a spring in my step and a lightness in my spirit. I was so thankful to have my sins washed away that I was eager to offer grace to others.

If I was upset with someone, it did become easier to imagine Jesus, looking compassionately on that person and on me, because as my momma would say, "two wrongs don't make a right." If I saw someone who was behaving badly, I could see the pain and love in Jesus' eyes. I certainly wanted Jesus to never give up on me, no matter how many times I would stumble, but I started to see that

He was just as long-suffering with those around me. Oh, my dear goodness! We all make bad choices time after time after time, don't we?

Our sins can define us, or they can motivate us to change. That's what God asks of us. He knows we are sinners. He knows we're going to stumble and make mistakes. He just wants us to remember that He loves us and that we can live with the confidence that we've been forgiven.

There is powerful influence wielded by a follower of Christ. It can be for good...or not. Do I live my life in such a way that others immediately discern that I'm His disciple *or* do I live my life like my baptism was in pickle juice? Do I behave saintly in front of my church friends and not-so-saintly in front of my other friends? Do I love my neighbor *and* do I forgive those who've hurt me? Do I gossip about my friend and hang on to past hurts like a security blanket, rationalizing my own sin of unforgiveness?

Folks, if I truly believe that there is power in the blood of Jesus, then I can't help but make every possible effort to be the face of unconditional love to those I meet each day. If I believe that Jesus took my sins with Him to the Cross, then I can't help but be the first to forgive others. If I believe the words in *Romans 6:1-5*, that sin is no longer my master, and I live under His grace, then I can't help but be joyful and hopeful.

Last year, Carrie Underwood released the song, *Something In The Water*. I saw it first on video and yes, I cried because of its exquisite imagery. Have you seen or heard it? If not, go buy it now. It is an astute observation of the unfathomable power, simplicity, and beauty of being washed clean. There *is* something in the water, and it's Jesus! When I met Him there, I was made new. I was changed. I was stronger. I was given the power of the Holy Spirit. I didn't become bullet-proof, but regarding eternity, death couldn't touch me. (cue MC Hammer and a smile)

I'm more than a little ashamed to say that I haven't given the Holy Spirit a chance to do all He can do in my life. With Him, there is more power than we can imagine, but I've put Him in a tiny box because I'm a little (okay, more than a little) afraid of where He might take me.

Anyone else afraid that God might take us up on the prayers we say and the songs we sing? Can I get an *Amen*?

I'm a work-in-progress, folks. I don't have all the answers, and I don't do it all just right. Oh, how I wish I did! For now, it has to be enough that, through Him, I'm redeemed and renewed. I hope you'll extend me some grace for the times I stumble because I have before and I will again.

That's just how it will go until I'm called Home.

I'm a Quitter

The title of this chapter was inspired by a sign that said, "I want to give up smoking, drinking, gambling and cursing, but I'm no quitter!"

After I had *quit* chuckling, it made me wonder what all I should *quit* doing.

Maybe, I should *quit* worrying about things (and people) I can't change. Maybe, I should *quit* being offended so easily. Maybe, I should *quit* expecting folks who don't believe in God to think, act and talk like those who do. Maybe, I should *quit* making excuses for not reading my Bible and spending time in prayer. Maybe, I should *quit* finding a reason for not loving my neighbor. Maybe, I should *quit* telling God how to run my life.

"Father, if you are willing, take this cup from me; yet not my will, but yours be done." -- Luke 22:42

(Maybe I should *quit* skipping over the scripture references that are in italics. I confess that I do that sometimes. I'll *quit*.)

Jesus was asking for relief, but He was willing to let God be in charge. He relinquished His will to God's will. Relinquish means abandon, surrender, yield...*quit*.

Life is hard. Sometimes, we feel like we did all the right things as we raised our kiddos and yet, we don't get the results we wanted. We fed them healthy food, we taught them about Jesus, and we made sure they buckled their seatbelts. Then, they get old enough to make their own choices and may not take care of their bodies or their souls. In my weaker moments, I assume the weight of their bad choices. (Like I always made good ones.)

What's up with teaching our children to be independent, to think for themselves and to be problem solvers? Good grief! They grow up to *do just that,* and I wish I'd just have said, "Because I said so, that's why."

Not really. Their dad and I taught them to be leaders and to make decisions. Sometimes, I don't especially care for all the decisions they make, but I am always thankful that they are not unwilling or incapable of living their own life. Goodness gracious, I don't want them living in our nest when they can soar on their own.

And it's not just about being a parent. We can do all the right things at church. We can be Bible class teachers and fill the communion trays.

We can do all the right things at work. We can make our sales quotas and complete all the blessed paperwork. (You know that's the hard part.)

We can do all the right things in our marriages. We can keep milk and Nestle' Quik on hand at all times.

And yet, we don't get the results we expected. Our efforts are not interpreted correctly and satan steps in with his lies. It happens.

Our church families have disagreements. We lose our job. Our spouse tells us he wants a divorce.

But it's not over till it's over. Prayer works. The Holy Spirit works. Don't listen to the devil's lies. Listen to God as He reminds you how much He loves you.

I've learned that the devil doesn't show up in my life with horns, a red cape, and a flaming pitchfork. He shows up with whatever appeals to me and then he lulls me into a false sense of security. The blanket that he brings to my party will be used to suffocate me. It will wrap around my fear, my hatred, my bitterness, my pain and my despair. It will hold those things next to me until I can't figure out how to throw them off...and I will die. (I'm preaching from experience here.) He means us no good. I had to search the

Word for myself to uncover the truth about unconditional love and forgiveness. Doing that put the devil on the run. Good riddance!

Submit yourselves, then, to God. Resist the devil, and he will flee from you. -- James 4:7

I am not a shopper; I am a purchaser. If I need a blouse, I go buy a blouse. I never just *go shopping* (shudder). However, as a young mom, I went with a friend so she could spend her Christmas money and so I could have some time out of the house with an adult. She wanted to check out the sales at Dillard's first. While we were there, we saw an older lady from church there, shopping. She was trying on a beautiful jacket, and it did look stunning on her. As she stood before the mirror, turning this way and that, she reached down to the price tag that was hanging from the sleeve. When she glanced at the price, she started removing the jacket and said, "Get thee behind me, satan!" She probably could have bought anything she wanted, but she knew when enough was enough. She taught this young mom the value of scripture in every moment of our lives.

The scripture she was referring to was *Matthew 16:23 - Jesus turned and said to Peter, "Get behind me, satan! You are a stumbling block to me; you do not have in mind the concerns of God, but merely human concerns."*

Jesus knew that He had to endure the Cross, and Peter was arguing with Him. Jesus told his friend to *quit* being a *stumbling block*. In giving this some thought, I wonder, do

I have in mind the concerns of God or merely my own selfish human concerns? Am I a stumbling block?

Quit asking me such hard questions!

At various times, I was in more pain than could have ever expected or imagined, and that pain seemed to be coming from every direction – home, work, and church. I tried to be courageous. I would look to the heavens and implore, "Can I just catch a break? Please?" I tried to catch my breath.

In an instant of clarity, the scripture came to mind that my Father in Heaven knows how to give good gifts. (Ask, seek, knock. Oh, yeah, *Matthew 7.*) Then, I began to pray courageously and boldly, asking the Creator of the Universe to give me wisdom, peace, comfort and hope. I pictured myself giving my child, husband, friend or boss to Him, and thereby releasing the expectation that I could fix it.

I can't. He can. In fact, His fix has been more than I could have hoped for in my family, even though it's all still a work-in-progress. *I'm* still a work-in-progress. Thank you, Jesus, for not giving up on me!

Please know that He hears our prayers and that His Spirit will show up with more might than we can comprehend. In the hardest moments of my life, God hasn't delivered me until I've given up; until I *quit*. He waits until I've thrown my hands up in exasperation and defeat...and then He delivers me. Maybe not like I wanted to be delivered, but He moves in my life, and He rescues me.

Just like Jesus, who said *"Father, if you are willing, take this cup from me; yet not my will, but yours be done."*

Today, I stand before you as a *quitter*. Lord, not my will, but Yours be done. I *quit*.

Iron Sharpens Iron

I've been in sales since I was about 11 years old when I was inspired by an ad in the back of my Archie comic book. Surely, you read the adventures of Archie and the gang from Riverdale High! There was Veronica, Betty, Jughead and that awful Reggie. Did you buy the sea monkeys for $1.25 from the ad inside the back cover? Or were you the nerd that spent a dollar on x-ray glasses? How about the stealthy secret agent periscope for fifty cents? Well, I chose to send off for a catalog to sell Christmas cards, door-to-door. I had my eye set on earning a beautiful gold watch pendant. I did just that and have been in sales ever since.

I've had opportunities to work with some talented people through the years. Some of my managers have been encouraging and inspiring, others have not. Some of my co-workers have been hard workers with a can-do attitude, others have not. I learned as much from the negative folks as I did from the positive ones.

We all go through a maze of trials and errors as we work our way from rookie to retiree. If we're ambitious, we look for ways to self-improve by taking classes and attending trainings. We update our wardrobe and expand our vocabulary. We find mentors, those people who have the qualities we'd like to have, and we begin to take on those best characteristics. Having mentors helps us learn from other people's mistakes.

Gotta love the time-saving involved in not having to personally make every mistake, right?

I've got several mentors relating to the various facets of my life: daughter, woman, wife, mother, worker, student. In every instance, these mentors have encouraged me to do my best by doing what was right, and if I messed up (which I certainly did), there was an encouragement to do better next time. It was an environment in which thriving success was more than possible, it was highly likely.

First of all, I have great parents that taught me that I could be anything just because I was Carrie. Their love and encouragement set a stable foundation that emboldened me to try new experiences. Their examples of working hard and playing hard gave me some great childhood memories. I'm surrounded by a large extended family, full of generous, loving folks who reinforced those lessons that I was learning at home.

I had teachers who made the extra effort to share life lessons, not just the subject at hand. Mrs. Jones was my 6th grade Bible class teacher and also my 6th grade school teacher. She put up with no nonsense from a bunch of rowdy twelve-year-olds, wherever we were. My family lived across the park from our church building, so it was easy to walk to Bible class on Sundays, where Mrs. Jones encouraged us to memorize scripture. The *Twenty-third Psalm* was on the learning list that year. I still recite that verse according to the King James Version.

The LORD is my shepherd; I shall not want. He maketh me to lie down in green pastures: he leadeth me beside the still waters. He restoreth my soul: he leadeth me in the paths of righteousness for his name's sake. Yea, though I walk through the valley of the shadow of death, I will fear no evil: for thou art with me; thy rod and thy staff they comfort me. Thou preparest a table before me in the presence of mine enemies: thou anointest my head with oil; my cup runneth over. Surely goodness and mercy shall follow me all the days of my life: and I will dwell in the house of the LORD forever.

It's comforting to recite such regal words. Who wouldn't want their soul to be restoreth and their cup to overfloweth?

As I was growing up, there were several women and men who set a good example for me to follow. There are others, but these particular folks are on my heart today.

Mrs. Fain would leave the air-conditioned comfort of her home to come outside and chat with the neighborhood kids. There were about a dozen of us between the ages of nine and thirteen that would ride bikes up and down those streets, between each other's houses for hours on end. She'd be out there, asking about our lives and taking mental notes. I remember her chatting with us about eternal life. She had those little booklets, called tracts, she would give us to take home and read. Talk about loving your neighbor!

Does anyone in your neighborhood do that? Mine either! (Note to self: get out of the recliner and go outside to chat with the neighborhood kids about things that matter.)

When I had a house full of babies, I'd go walking with the ladies in the neighborhood after getting our little darlings in bed for the night. We ranged in age from twenty-ish to fifty-something. As we walked, we talked about everything – kids, husbands, parents, recipes and God. Their wise counsel was good for me mentally and spiritually. The exercise was good for me physically. You can't beat that triple play!

Once I entered the workforce and chose a telecom career, I was working with David and Wayne, two men of excellent character, who also happened to be a couple of characters. Working with happy folks doesn't seem so much like work, does it?

David was my manager, so he got the unenviable task of trying to tame and harness the energy of an unpredictable whirlwind. When I think back to the person I was then, and how I acted, it makes me cringe. Picture an annoying, stereotypical salesperson - that was me. I was pushy, loud and competitive at all costs with an I-know-it-all-so-you-can't-teach-me-anything attitude. My co-workers were less than impressed, I can assure you.

I've asked David many times: "Why did you put up with me?" and "Why didn't you just kill me and tell God that I died?" He says that he saw potential in me. I'm glad he could see through all that muddy water. More than that, I appreciate that he took the time to invest in me, not because it would get him where he wanted to be in his career, but to help me get to where I wanted to be in mine.

Over the years, with a sharp knife carefully cutting away the undesirable traits, I learned to be an atypical sales person. I'm not pushy, loud nor a cut-throat competitor. There's enough business out there for all of us. I have come to appreciate that coaching combined with honing my skills works in my favor.

Wayne was the installer of the telecom stuff I sold, so we spent many, many traveling hours discussing profound ideas like the definition of truth and how to achieve world peace. Wayne sees things in two colors: right and wrong. He isn't afraid to tell it like it is. I was susceptible to rationalizing my situational ethics, so it was a learning experience for me to be with someone who never even considered being swayed by a whim.

As a wife and mom with a full-time job, I was always having some kind of a crisis, as you've read here. Wayne was always calm and said wise things like "I'll pray for you. Sometimes people say that like it's the last option, but if I had thirteen hands, I couldn't do better for you than to pray for you." Now, isn't that the truth?!

I started to enjoy writing when I was in junior high. For the next few years, I wrote poems as I rode the roller coaster of teenage angst. I was either dancing with joy (groovy, like on American Bandstand) or writhing in agony (similar to the melting death of the Wicked Witch of the West). Oh, brother.

As I matured in my faith, I began to hunger for deeper biblical knowledge. I dreamed that I could be an author and professional speaker one day. To learn as much as possible, I applied to the Sunset School of Preaching to begin taking classes in the Fall of 1992. Sunset is primarily a training ground for the menfolk to become pulpit ministers. I was the only woman applying to be in the classes that term.

I received my form acceptance letter in the mail, addressed to Mr. Carrie Blair. In part, the letter read: *It will be a thrill to watch you grow into a man prepared for this divine task.*

Grow into a man?!

I laughed. I showed the letter to my husband, and he said something to the effect of "Yikes!" as he laughed. We showed the letter to our friends, and they laughed, too.

Not one to let a good joke go to waste, I composed a letter to the school's director that began:

It is with a humorous disposition that I write to you concerning the letter of acceptance I received from you and the Sunset instructors. Your letter arrived addressed to Mr. Carrie Blair. After I had read the context of the letter, I came to realize that the "Mr." was prophetic. I am not a woman that is offended with the masculine voice being used in modern communication. However, I must admit that I am concerned about the sentence that reads, "It will be a thrill to watch you grow into a man..." My husband and I are curious about this change. Please advise as to the date of this spectacle since my husband, our family and friends will want to take the day off to watch. We are recharging the video camera's battery now.

I sent copies of both letters to one of Mr. Paden's close friends, and I'm absolutely certain there was some good-natured joking. When I introduced myself at Orientation, the director just grinned and said, "Oh, it's you."

Later, I heard Mr. Paden say, "We all have a purpose, and I am 100% convinced that nothing on this earth can take us if we have not fulfilled that purpose. By the same token, when we have completed our purpose, nothing on this earth can keep us here."

Let that sink in for a bit.

That's heady stuff, isn't it? It bears repeating that we serve at the pleasure of the King, and we will serve Him on Earth until He calls us Home.

During my time at Sunset, my favorite classes were the Bible History classes with Richard Rogers. He brought the Old Testament to life with all the drama and excitement of a novel. He inspired us to become familiar with the stories and then apply the lessons in our lives. For those who've been led to believe the Bible doesn't make sense unless you're a scholar, please try reading it again, because it is a marvelous story, full of adventure, comedy, heartache and victory!

The studying, training, and course-correction are not intended to be pleasant, but the end result is to become better than before. Imagine the clanking of iron upon iron as the sword's dull edge is honed to become sharp. If that edge remains dull, it is worthless to fulfill the purpose for which it was created.

As iron sharpens iron, so one person sharpens another.
--Proverbs 27:17

I cannot be thankful enough that I was able to surround myself with people that pointed me in the right direction, that didn't give or take excuses, and that set a good example in their work ethic; people who didn't tell me what I wanted to hear, but told me the truth and encouraged me toward fine-tuning my skills and behaviors.

It is my earnest desire that I have been that person for others who needed some coaching. In my experience, most folks aren't looking for a handout; they are looking for a hand up.

The best we can do is offer someone grace and courage. There may be something to this.

Sing and be Happy

In August of 1998, a friend said, "Tell me about Carrie." I shared a few milestones and stories. As I did that, it occurred to me: If the Maker of Heaven and Earth had told me to pick anything I wanted in my life, I wouldn't have chosen as many good things as I have received. I'd have never considered asking for a marriage that is this solid. I'd have never contemplated having such a loving and fun family. These things were not on my radar. Even with all the trials, the pain, and the loss, I'm thankful for the life I have and the people I have in it. What kind of shape would we be in if I had kept dragging that big ol' rock and living a life of fear, shame and guilt? I'm grateful that I'll never know.

The Bible has a story about a prophet named Jonah. The book begins *"The word of the Lord came to Jonah..."*. By verse three of the first chapter, we read, *"But Jonah ran away from the Lord."* He ran to a ship. God sent a great wind on the sea that tossed that ship around. Jonah tells his shipmates, "Pick me up and throw me into the sea, and it will become calm. I know that it is my fault that this great storm has come upon us." Jonah is thrown overboard. The Lord provided a great fish to swallow Jonah and Jonah was inside the fish three days and three nights, praying.

Sometimes God figuratively provides a great storm and a great fish to get my attention. Then I spend three days and three nights praying, ultimately concluding that maybe God knows best. Then, like Jonah, I sing a song of thanksgiving and proclaim that salvation comes from the Lord.

Once the storm is over, I sometimes forget the lesson I'd hoped to have learned.

Let's see what David has to share in *Psalm 139:1-12*
You have searched me, LORD, and you know me. You know when I sit and when I rise; you perceive my thoughts from afar. You discern my going out and my lying down; you are familiar with all my ways. Before a word is on my tongue you, LORD, know it completely. You hem me in behind and before, and you lay your hand upon me. Such knowledge is too wonderful for me, too lofty for me to attain.

Where can I go from your Spirit? Where can I flee from your presence? If I go up to the heavens, you are there; if I make my bed in the depths, you are there. If I rise on the wings of the dawn, if I settle on the far side of the sea, even there your hand will guide me, your right hand will hold me fast. If I say, "Surely the darkness will hide me, and the light become night around me," even the darkness will not be dark to you; the night will shine like the day, for darkness is as light to you.

I can see myself in these stories. Do I prefer hiding in the dark and doing things my way or am I willing to trust God and come into His light and live as if He'd set me free from my chains? What would it take for me to make that change? The Father of Lies means us no good. Ever. Am I still listening to him?

God loves us enough to pursue us, to tap us on the shoulder and point out that He always has been and will always be the Great I Am.

Jesus said, *"Come to me, all you who are weary and burdened, and I will give you rest. Take my yoke upon you and learn from me, for I am gentle and humble in heart, and you will find rest for your souls. For my yoke is easy and my burden is light." -- Matthew 11:28-30*

Jesus asks us to come to Him, and He will give us rest from our burdens. He is gentle and humble in heart. I think that sounds so peaceful and refreshing. What will be my response to Him? Will I run *or* will I surrender, day after day after day?

Sometimes in worship, I catch myself singing mindlessly because I know the words to many of the songs. I am convicted that *maybe I need to pay attention* when singing to my Lord. I wonder if I even believe what I'm singing. With these songs, I am praying, promising, surrendering, repenting, affirming and loving. These melodies and lyrics, wafting from my lips, heart and hands are a sacrificial offering which I sincerely hope are a sweet aroma to my Breath of Life.

I love the depth of meaning found in the old hymns. *Blessed Assurance* is one of my favorites. It was written by Fanny J. Crosby, an American hymn writer and poetess who lived from 1820 to 1915 and wrote about 9,000 hymns. *Nine thousand hymns.* Oh yeah, and she was blind. She was often asked to perform for presidents, generals and other dignitaries, even playing for President Grant's funeral. Though she was a teacher and a prolific poem and hymn writer, her passionate life's work was helping the poor and needy. Check out the words she chose to convey her absolute confidence in her Savior:

Blessed assurance, Jesus is mine!
Oh, what a foretaste of glory divine!
Heir of salvation, purchase of God,
born of His Spirit, washed in His blood.

Perfect submission, perfect delight,
visions of rapture now burst on my sight;
Angels descending, bring from above
echoes of mercy, whispers of love.

Perfect submission, all is at rest,
I in my Saviour am happy and blest;
Watching and waiting, looking above,
filled with His goodness, lost in His love.

This is my story, this is my song,
Praising my Saviour all the day long;
This is my story, this is my song,
Praising my Saviour all the day long.

So I ask myself, *am I watching and waiting, looking above, filled with His goodness, lost in His love?*

And there are other songs. *Do I believe that Jesus loves me and that I am weak, but He is strong? Do I, in awesome wonder, consider all the worlds His hands have made? Do I want Him to abide in me?*

I sure hope that the answer to all these questions is a resounding *YES*.

Music touches us on many physical and spiritual levels. The melodies and lyrics can sooth us, excite us or embolden us. Music can magically transport us to another time and place. When we hear a certain song, we can remember where we were, who we were with and what we were feeling.

I remember being pregnant with my first child in the early 80's and singing along to the Beach Boys' *Little Deuce Coupe* on the stereo as I was cooking supper. I happened to remember that the Beach Boys had been around since before I was born, and then this thought flitted through my consciousness: my mother was probably singing along to the Beach Boys when she was pregnant with me. I felt connected to all the formerly pregnant mommies on my family tree who were part of me being born.

Aahhh, the circle of life.

I also imagined that I was having a pretty easy time cooking supper, compared to those back up the line who went out in the yard to grab a chicken to fry, then went down to the root cellar to grab a few potatoes and a jar of homemade peach preserves. Maybe a book about those stories will come later.

Ahem. Back to the music.

I had aspirations of being a famous recording artist when, as a ten-year-old schoolgirl, I would sit in my room and sing along with Olivia Newton John's hit, *Have You Never Been Mellow*. When I was about fourteen, I would sing along with much volume and no regret to the Bee Gees during my Saturday morning chores. I was *More Than a Woman* as I was *Stayin' Alive* long enough to get that *Night Fever*. (Did you see what I did there?!) And as a bonus, the upbeat tempo helped me clean the house in record time.

I still clean house to loud, happy music blaring from the surround sound speakers. If you don't, you should try it at least once.

No doubt, my love of singing came from my paternal genes. My dad grew up in a large farming family who loved to sing. Dad was the youngest of ten kids. The story is told that as all of the family was working on the crops in the fields, they would sing. Neighbors a half-mile away could hear their choir. Keep in mind, they didn't have a piano or guitar in the fields with them, so they all lifted their voices in four-part harmony. What an amazing God we have, who created us with such magnificent instruments as our vocal chords, our fingers, our hearts, and our minds.

This family of singers was pretty good, from what I've heard, because they were asked to sing for funerals and other events. Sometimes, there was a *singing,* which was a gathering where they...sang. The Goheen family would enjoy popular musical groups of the day, like The Stamps, The Ozarks, the Blackwood Brothers and the Carter Family (as in June Carter Cash, her momma, and sister). My granddad, Pop, even penned several hymns, a couple of which were published.

Dad sang with a group from church in the early 1970's. I can remember a few Sunday evenings that we would go to one of the singer's home and have a potluck supper. Then, they would sit at the dining table, rehearsing the songs: *Sing and Be Happy, Just a Little Talk With Jesus, If We Never Meet Again* and others.

As is often the case, I didn't realize then what I was witnessing when I was such a young girl. Those memories have brought me much joy over the years, and those particular songs have been a salve for my soul on more than one occasion. At Daddy's funeral, we played a couple of those recorded songs, and I expect that if he could see us, he laughed. He loved making people smile, and he'd have liked singing at his own funeral.

There are all kinds of hymns. Some are prayers, others are praise, and still others are about the hope of heaven. I'm confident that, when he was singing the songs for the album, Dad had no idea the legacy he would leave for his children--a legacy of singing and being happy, talking to Jesus and longing for heaven.

Because I enjoy singing, we'd get all our little darlings in bed at night, then I'd sit on the floor in the hallway with a hymnal in hand and sing them to sleep. (I know you're wondering, but no, I didn't steal the hymnal from the church.) It was a peaceful end to their day and mine. I hope those precious moments are embedded in their souls for eternity, as they are in mine.

Jesus loves me, this I know, for the Bible tells me so.

Next time I'm singing, I'll pay attention to what I'm saying. It doesn't matter if the song is pop, rap, country or gospel. Is this a message I want to send? Am I comfortable with the words and their meaning?

Go look up the lyrics to the songs we sing along with while we're cruising down the road of life. I did, and it surprised me. It embarrassed me! I would never say those things, but I sure have been singing those words. I've been foolish by being inattentive to my own words. I am now more aware of all that I allow into my mind, whether it is on the radio, television or the computer. Those words and images matter.

This is a compelling reason to listen to quality radio content. Personally, I have Air1, KLOVE, Family Life, American Family, Rejoice plus a couple of local Christian contemporary radio stations preset into my car's radio. I love jamming (is that still valid terminology?) and praising God as I travel the highways and byways for our frequent road trips. There are other worthwhile listening options. I'll always be a fan of country music, especially the old stuff. I love me some Statler Brothers, probably because the harmonious voices are so engaging and familiar to me.

The story is told of John Newton, who was a servant to a ship captain in the year 1747. Although his mother had given her very young son some religious instruction before her death, John held no religious convictions. On the ship's journey toward home, there was a great storm and John feared the ship would sink. What did he do? He prayed for deliverance. The ship was saved, and he marked that as his spiritual conversion.

How many times have I asked God to deliver me from a mess that I've gotten myself into? I haven't kept count, but it's a bunchy bunchy!

So, I consider the words that John Newton crafted into a song to illustrate a sermon in 1773:
Amazing Grace! (How sweet the sound)
That saved a wretch like me!
I once was lost, but now I'm found;
was blind, but now I see.

'Twas grace that taught my heart to fear,
and grace my fears relieved.
How precious did that grace appear
the hour I first believed!

Through many dangers, toils and snares
I have already come.
'Tis grace hath brought me safe this far,
and grace will lead me home.

The Lord has promised good to me,
His word my hope secures;
He will my shield and portion be,
as long as life endures.

Yes, when this flesh and heart shall fail,
and mortal life shall cease;
I shall possess, within the veil,
a life of joy and peace.

The earth shall soon dissolve like snow,
the sun forbear to shine;
But God, who called me here below,
will be forever mine.

When we've been there ten thousand years,
bright shining as the sun,
we've no less days to sing God's praise
than when we first begun.

Verses have been added through the years, which lend depth to the wonder of God's amazing grace towards a sinner like me. I can't understand it, but I am so thankful for it. The old hymns say more than you'd expect with their economy of words.

I pray that we all will surrender our burden to the Rock of Ages; that we'll let Him love us; that we'll let His Spirit convict us and use us to suit His purpose for our lives.

Philippians 2:13 tells us "...for it is God who works in you to will and to act in order to fulfill his good purpose."

God works in us.

In us. Wow!

You Know that You're My Favorite

My favorite memories of raising our family involve yummy food and boisterous laughter. How about you? Did you have family reunions and Fourth of July parties with crazy relatives and friends? I prize the times we spent living and loving, especially if there was homemade peach ice cream on the menu.

We share the stories that begin "I remember when..." and we find out who our parents and grandparents were when they were younger. We hear our parents' friends tell about pranks (like letting the Ag show pigs loose in the school building) and playing hooky from school (or Bible class – you know who you are). We become a part of their story, and they become a part of ours.

To my way of thinking, it is significant to cultivate meaningful relationships for ourselves and our families. The friends I have had through the years made all the difference in my life and in my family's lives. By choosing to be surrounded by groovy people of rock-solid faith, excellent character, and high expectations, we became *more* than we might have otherwise.

Friends love through all kinds of weather, and families stick together in all kinds of trouble.
--Proverbs 17:17 (The Message)

Hanging out with good folks can bolster, inspire and encourage good character. Think about the friends you have. Do they make you *more* than you already are or do they chip away at you? Man, oh man. I've had those who chipped away at me, and it was not a pretty sight.

There are a handful of friends that I consider my *inner circle*. They can be brutally honest if I need some coaching. They can be trusted to not gossip. They share my sorrow and double my joy. They know my strengths and weaknesses, and I know theirs, but we shower each other with grace, acceptance and love.

And protection.

I met Barb the first day of first grade, and she was my very best friend from the beginning. She served as my Maid of Honor when I married Mr. B and now is the artist that creates my signature hairstyle (silver and spiky). She has been the best friend a gal could have through all these years, and I dearly love her and her family. I've always known she was tough enough to whip me, so it's been advantageous to have her on my side.

When I was especially vulnerable (read: an emotionally raw, sobbing mess) at the visitation before my Dad's funeral, Barb came and sat through the whole thing with her husband, dad, and brother, just being there, in case I needed her. What a devoted friend. Can I pick 'em, or what?

The family friends we have had over the years hold a special place in my heart. These godly men and women have mentored and encouraged the Blair kids and loved them as their own. Their investment in us has paid more dividends than I could have imagined. Again, they made us *more* than we already were. When we build relationships that span decades of events: birth, death, joy, heartache and large doses of fun and laughter, we make a rich life. Who, in their right mind, would want to miss that?

Back in 1989, I had a seven-, six-, four- and two-year-old. My friend, Jane, had four kids the same ages, and we were always taking turns babysitting because it was honestly easier to have all eight than just our four. They lived next to a church. This particular day, Jane looked out the front window to check on the little darlings. There was a funeral at the church, and the cars were lined up down the street for the procession. All eight of the kids were standing on the curb, waving and hollering "Parade! Parade!" at the passing cars. Since they were used to small-town parades, they were a little miffed that no one was throwing candy out the car windows for them. Jane was mortified, but she noticed, as she corralled the young 'uns, that everyone in the cars was smiling at these cute kids. This is a favorite memory for everyone in both families and probably the folks in the funeral procession.

Because we had all eight kiddos together most of the time, she had a van, and I had a suburban. When we'd leave each other's house, we'd do a roll call to make sure we had all our kids. More than once, she got home and was unloading her brood, but found she had a stowaway Blair kid, so she loaded them all back into her van and brought the little rascal back home.

When I'd do a roll call, it was in the chronological order of birth. One hot afternoon when I had all eight of the little darlings, we loaded up to go to town for Happy Hour at Sonic. I started backing out of the drive and heading down the road as I called the roll. When I got to Landon, the other kids said, "He's not here." This was an old trick, and I wasn't falling for it...again, so I kept driving. The kids were hollering by now, "Landon's not here!"

Don't call the authorities; I was less than a half-mile away from home when I turned around and went back to find Landon, locked safely inside my house. It took about twenty years for him to forgive me. There were a little "reap what you sow" and "the boy who cried wolf" lessons in this story for all of our little imps.

Mercy! What you can learn from having lots of kids and hanging out with folks who have lots of kids, too.

For a summer money-making project, the kids made paper airplanes and sold them door-to-door for a nickel apiece. What great neighbors we had. I was so proud to be handing down the family legacy of salesmanship.

There was the time Ashley and Josh, ages five and four, climbed up on the cabinet to get the key to the storage building. They got out the spray paint and proceeded to write their names *on the neighbor's brick house*. I love it when little ones write on the walls and such because all they know is how to write their own name. Busted! Judge me as you will, but this is what happens when you are nursing a baby, and you think the other kids are playing quietly. They *were* playing quietly. Lesson learned.

Moving from Levelland was traumatic for all of us, but it meant being closer to Steve's work so that we got to see him more often. We made new friends and got involved with a new church family.

When I asked the kids about their favorite memories, it struck me that our choosing to have four children meant we had a built-in Fun House. We always ate dinner together, which wasn't always easy, but it was always worth it. When we had little ones, we brought a towel with us to the dinner table because it wasn't a matter of *if* there was going to be a spill, but *when* there was going to be a spill.

There was even an emergency room trip that originated at the dinner table when cute little Josh put a pinto bean up his nose. I can still see that worried look on his face as he wiped his nose over and over. I asked, "Josh, what's wrong?" He was silent. Steve tried to interrogate him and then it dawned on both of us: a bean! He stuck a bean up his nose! He was too little to "blow" his nose, so we were afraid that he would suck that bean up higher if we asked him to blow it out.

The kids fondly remember the diesel-engine suburban that had to be plugged in during the winter months so that it would start each morning. They and their friends referred to it as The Burb, and it was a rolling navy-blue ball of power. We took it to deliver them to summer camp and on youth trips to Six Flags because it was roomy. We used those youth trips as our family vacations most summers. We went to Six Flags about 8 years in a row in The Burb, with the music cranked up as we made wacky, amusing memories.

When the kids were teens, we lived in a house in the country that didn't have a bright light outside at night, so it was very dark. The boys had us take them to an Army surplus store, where they bought camo attire. Our whole family and any friends who were there, would dress in black or camo, then play Hide 'n Seek. It was incredible! It was so dark that if you had on dark gloves and hid your face, someone would walk right by you. There was running, screaming and hysterical laughter.

Good times. No, *great times*!

When we gathered in early July for several years with a few other families, there are stories of fifteen kids and not-so-safe fireworks at 4th of July events. It's a wonder we never had to call an ambulance. What one kid didn't think of, the next one would. And of course, even the worst idea sounds like a stroke of genius when there are fourteen co-conspirators to fan the flame.

We spent Sunday lunches at the pizza place that had a special deal where two kids could eat for free with each adult meal purchase. *That* was nice. After each six-week report card came out, the kids would get game tokens for good grades, and we'd spend a little extra time in the game room on those Sundays. It was usually the dads who had a hard time pulling themselves away from the arcade games. Getting older is mandatory, but growing up is optional, apparently.

Our congregation had a one day VBS each summer, called Bible Bonanza. Our whole family participated by acting, teaching or helping. There were silly songs and authentic costumes used to convey important Bible stories, but I think the best part is that all six of us were using our various gifts as we participated in the Broadway-quality production. Ok, maybe not Broadway-quality, but it was brilliantly creative and well-performed. To make all that even better, we were with other families who were doing the same thing.

As empty nesters, most weeks will find us sharing Game Night with one of our couple friends. We play spirited games of Cards & Marbles, where we pit the guys against the girls in some good-natured trash-talk while drawing cards, moving our marbles around the board and strategically (or just for fun) "killing" some marbles and sending them back to Start. We can decompress and catch up on each other's lives. We solve the problems of the universe while we visit, no doubt.

There are dozens of stories that our family shares with those who have been brave enough to wade through life with us. It's really amazing, and I'd do it all over again.

Well, most of it.

Of course, meaningful friendships can come from your family members because we share blood and DNA. For many of us, our siblings and our cousins are our first best friends. A few years ago, some of my cousins were together for a weekend. As we were standing around together to say our goodbyes, Jane told the cousin nearest her, "It was so good to see you," then she leaned forward and in a stage whisper said, "You know you're my favorite." From there, she went to the next one and said, "You look wonderful, and it's so great to be with my (stage whisper) *favorite* cousin." This was repeated to each and every one of us. It was hilarious! And, it was true. We are all her favorites for one reason or another. Now, all these cousins say it every time we talk. They really are my favorite (and I'm theirs). Oh, how I love them all.

I have fun memories of my cousin picking me up after school on Friday and letting me spend the weekend with her. She let me paint with watercolors. My mom didn't do watercolors. (To be fair, my kid's mom didn't do watercolors, either. Bahahahaha!)

Our inner circle changes as we go through school and move on to have our own families.

One valuable reason to maintain long relationships is to make sure the childhood secrets get kept. It's a matter of *honor among thieves* when we keep quiet about the mysteriously thrown water balloons and they keep quiet about maybe sneaking a few contraband cigarettes.

Shhhh. Don't tell our parents, please!

A large part of building those amazing relationships starts with us being *real*. To find a friend, I must first be a friend. We all need friends who can be called on in the middle of the night to help; the kind of aid that might require waking to pray or rolling up shirt sleeves to work or sitting on the floor to cry or making a trip to 7-11 for some ginger ale and crackers.

On the best of days, we need someone to join us in silly shenanigans (cue Lucy and Ethel). Maybe that means dressing up in 50's attire, going to the Sonic for a cheeseburger and a chocolate shake, then going to 50's Night at the local music theater. Yep, we did that. Elvis was even with us. Who wants to be normal when *groovy* and *weird* are options?

Maybe that means loudly harmonizing with *Lyin' Eyes* or doing your best impression of Jerry Lee belting out *Great Balls of Fire*. Or maybe that means learning every song on the *My Best Friend's Wedding* soundtrack while on a road trip, then going to see that movie at the theater and singing along to the whole thing. Yep, been there. Done that. I don't even want to know what the other movie-goers were thinking.

Ok, I gotta stop because there are just too many songs and too little ink. You get the picture. It's all about sharing life. Real life. Corny, goofball fun that made me laugh till my stomach muscles ached. It's all just the best. The. Best.

Those who choose to be in my life's line of fire have witnessed it all. That goes both ways. We've seen each other at our jubilant, victorious best, and we have seen each other at our worst, most desperate, wailing selves. Life can be messy. Life can be a blast.

Choose your accomplices wisely. Then be a favorite.

Try to be Ugly

Have you met someone and you just *knew* they had surrendered to Jesus? We live in the Bible Belt, where almost everyone we come into contact with has, at least, heard of Jesus. I have personally never met someone who has never heard of Jesus. So, if this is a Jesus-saturated area of the *world*, have all of us surrendered to Jesus? Have we gotten complacent and just assumed that *Matthew 28:18-20* has already happened here?

I'm afraid that we still find ways to use the Bible as a weapon rather than an instrument of peace and love. Our neighbors can't see that we have surrendered to Jesus, because we have become judge and jury to everyone we meet, measuring them with a ruler that we sure wouldn't want to be used on ourselves.

What would happen if we chose to love with abandon; if we chose to offer extravagant grace; if we chose to forgive instantly; if we chose to live a life that overflows with joy and hope? What would that look like?

I'd like to find out! Wouldn't it be fun?

I was privileged to see Bob Goff, the author of "Love Does," last year at a dinner for Lubbock Christian University. In his book, he shares stories from his life in which he chose to actively love others. An enthusiastic Bob smiles a giant smile, hugs you and tells you he is glad to have met you. He smiled at me. He hugged me. He lives like he's been forgiven and like he believes that God is love. Bob is love in action.

I think Jesus would have done the very same thing if I'd met Him. I think Jesus *will* do the very same thing *when* I meet Him.

During his presentation, Bob said, "When someone meets us, they should feel like they've just met Jesus; like they've just seen Heaven." He also said, "Love everybody. Always."

He is especially talking about those folks who are mentioned in Matthew 25. They are hungry, thirsty, homeless, naked, sick and incarcerated. These dear-to-Jesus folks take us outside of our comfort zone and make us squirm just a little bit. What happens if I go on up and love them? Maybe when I walk away, they will say to themselves, "I wonder if that's what Heaven looks like?"

We can live forgiven and love like that.

I pray that our encounters with God's love will fill us to overflowing and that we will be transformed by His love in such a way that we can't help but love everyone we see. Everyone.

This is a long passage where Jesus gives us some pointers on how to treat others:

"But to you who are listening, I say: Love your enemies, do good to those who hate you, bless those who curse you, pray for those who mistreat you. If someone slaps you on one cheek, turn to them the other also. If someone takes your coat, do not withhold your shirt from them. Give to everyone who asks you, and if anyone takes what belongs to you, do not demand it back. Do to others as you would have them do to you.

"If you love those who love you, what credit is that to you? Even sinners love those who love them. And if you do good to those who are good to you, what credit is that to you? Even sinners do that. And if you lend to those from whom you expect repayment, what credit is that to you? Even sinners lend to sinners, expecting to be repaid in full. But love your enemies, do good to them, and lend to them without expecting to get anything back. Then your reward will be great, and you will be children of the Most High because he is kind to the ungrateful and wicked. Be merciful, just as your Father is merciful.

"Do not judge, and you will not be judged. Do not condemn, and you will not be condemned. Forgive, and you will be forgiven. Give, and it will be given to you. A good measure, pressed down, shaken together and

running over, will be poured into your lap. For with the measure you use, it will be measured to you."
-- Luke 6:27-38

I want to use a fair measuring rod so that same mercy will come back to me. Sometimes, I forget that, and I become self-righteous and indignant when I've been wronged. The world nudges me in the side and whispers, "Hey! Don't let them get away with that!" But I know that my puffing up and getting in a tizzy is never the answer. It's what I want to do, for sure. But, as I get older (and hopefully wiser) I know it isn't the best answer. I pray that God always gently guides me back to His way (even when I deserve a smack on the backside).

I'm making a concentrated attempt to stop going back to my old habits of acting like I haven't been forgiven. It happens when I trip over my holier-than-thou attitude and act like I'm all that and a bag of chips. I've seen the story below several times in various forms, but the unknown author drives home the Bible stories we've heard all our lives:

Sometimes, do you wonder why God called you to do something for Him? There are many reasons why God shouldn't have called you, or me, or anyone else for that matter, but God doesn't wait until we are perfect to call us. Think of all those whom God has used. You're in good company if you think you aren't ready for God to use.

- *Abraham lied.*
- *Sarah laughed at God's promises.*
- *Moses stuttered.*

- *David's armor didn't fit.*
- *John Mark was rejected by Paul.*
- *Timothy had ulcers.*
- *Hosea's wife was a prostitute.*
- *Amos' training was in the school of fig-tree pruning.*
- *Jacob was a liar.*
- *David had an affair.*
- *Solomon was too rich.*
- *Jesus was too poor.*
- *Abraham was too old.*
- *David was too young.*
- *Peter was afraid of death.*
- *Lazarus was dead.*
- *John was self-righteous.*
- *Naomi was a widow.*
- *Paul and Moses were murderers.*
- *Jonah ran from God.*
- *Miriam was a gossip.*
- *Gideon and Thomas both doubted.*
- *Jeremiah was depressed and suicidal.*
- *Elijah was burned out.*
- *John the Baptist was a loudmouth.*
- *Martha was a worry-wart.*
- *Mary may have been lazy.*
- *Samson had long hair.*
- *Noah got drunk.*
- *Moses, Peter, Paul, and others had a short fuse.*

But God doesn't hire and fire like most bosses because He's more like our Dad than a boss. He doesn't look at financial gain or loss. He's not prejudiced or partial, nor sassy and brassy, nor deaf to our cry. He's not blind to our faults. His gifts to us are free. We could do wonderful things for others and still not be wonderful ourselves. The evil one says, "You're not worthy!" Jesus says, "So what? I AM." The evil one looks back and sees our mistakes. God looks back and sees the Cross.

We are made in His image. So is everyone we meet each day. That person that creeps me out? Yep, made in the image of God. That relative that wronged me? Yep, made in the image of God. That person who is obviously content to be living a life of sin? Yep, made in the image of God. That realization sure changes how I view others.

Ugly, the cat
Everyone in the apartment complex where I lived knew who Ugly was. Ugly was the resident tomcat. Ugly loved three things in this world: fighting, eating garbage, and shall we say, love.

The combination of these things combined with a life spent outside had their effect on Ugly. To start with, he had only one eye and where the other should have been was a hole. He was also missing his ear on the same side, his left foot appeared to have been badly broken at one time, and had healed at an unnatural angle, making him look like he was always turning the corner.

Ugly would have been a dark gray tabby, striped-type, except for the sores covering his head, neck, and even his *shoulders. Every time someone saw Ugly, there was the same reaction. "That's one UGLY cat!!!"*

All the children were warned not to touch him, the adults threw rocks at him, hosed him down, squirted him when he tried to come in their homes or shut his paws in the door when he would not leave.

Ugly always had the same reaction. If you turned the hose on him, he would stand there, getting soaked until you gave up and quit. If you threw things at him, he would curl his lanky body around your feet in forgiveness. Whenever he spied children, he would come running, meowing frantically and bump his head against their hands, begging for their love. If you picked him up, he would immediately begin suckling on your shirt, earrings, whatever he could find.

One day Ugly shared his love with the neighbor's huskies. They did not respond kindly, and Ugly was badly mauled. From my apartment, I could hear his screams, and I tried to rush to his aid. By the time I got to where he was laying, it was apparent Ugly's sad life was almost at an end.

As I picked him up and tried to carry him home, I could hear him wheezing and gasping, and could feel him struggling. I must be hurting him terribly, I thought.

Then I felt a familiar tugging, sucking sensation on my ear - Ugly, in so much pain, suffering and obviously dying, was trying to suckle my ear. I pulled him closer to me, and he bumped the palm of my hand with his head, then he turned one golden eye towards me, and I could hear the distinct sound of purring. Even in the greatest pain, that ugly battled-scarred cat was asking only for a little affection, perhaps some compassion.

At that moment, I thought Ugly was the most beautiful, loving creature I had ever seen. Never once did he try to bite or scratch me, try to get away from me, or struggle in any way. Ugly just looked up at me completely trusting in me to relieve his pain.

Ugly died in my arms before I could get inside, but I sat and held him for a long time afterward, thinking about how one scarred, deformed little stray could so alter my opinion about what it means to have true pureness of spirit, to love so totally and truly. Ugly taught me more about giving and compassion than a thousand books, lectures, or talk show specials ever could, and for that, I will always be thankful.

He had been scarred on the outside, but I was scarred on the inside, and it was time for me to move on and learn to love truly and deeply. To give my total to those I cared for.

Many people want to be richer, more successful, well liked, beautiful, but for me, I will always try to be Ugly. – Author Unknown

I include Ugly's story here because I am scared on the inside, too. In retrospect, I know that I'm guilty of having judged people by their label, appearance, and/or behavior. I was wrong to do that. I repent for having an ugly spirit toward some of God's children who didn't look or act like I thought they should. Like I was a paragon of virtue, and it was my job to wield the golden gavel. Good grief!

With the tongue, we praise our Lord and Father, and with it, we curse human beings, who have been made in God's likeness. Out of the same mouth come praise and cursing. My brothers and sisters, this should not be.
-- James 3:9-10

If anyone thinks they're too damaged to be beautiful or useful, please think again. I'm ever so grateful that light shines best through the pots with the most cracks. I've got enough of those groovy cracks that Jesus can't help but shine through. God's grace is more than enough to handle any weaknesses. Jesus heals. Jesus redeems. Jesus restores.

Grasp His grace with both hands and refuse to let it slip away.

Folks, I promise that as I head into the future, I'll endeavor to love everyone I see, and I'll let God take care of holding them accountable. I'll lay aside the prejudice, blaming, and shaming to focus on letting my life overflow with love and joy and hope so that everyone I meet will know they've seen Heaven.

Obligatory Slop

Yea! I'm the parent of a teenager, and I get to go on summer youth mission trips as a sponsor!

Stephen and I took turns going on the summer youth mission trips. One summer in the late '90s, it was my turn to go. That particular mission trip took us to The Fortress in downtown Ft Worth. It is a church that offers food, clothing and Jesus to the homeless.

It was the hottest summer I could remember, and since we were in Ft Worth, it was so humid, I thought I was going to die. I worked with the team that was cleaning out a food pantry that had been infested with rodents. Yep, a pleasant job and ideal circumstances – not! Others cleaned up and repaired needy houses and overgrown yards while others sorted donated clothes by size and gender. All of it was hot, dirty work. And I do mean work. Why did we do this? Because we wanted to show the love of Christ to those who were down and out. We all find ourselves needing a hand up at some time our lives.

A secondary goal was to give all these youth group teens a chance to see how others live. We had to pack for a week in a drawstring laundry-type bag. Each morning, we had to re-pack and take our bags with us, as if we were homeless and had to keep all our earthly possessions with us at all times. We had breakfast in the dorm, but for lunch and supper, we went to different places that offered food to the homeless. We ate what was offered to us, and we visited with the other folks eating there.

One of the places we went was by the railroad tracks with some abandoned loading docks, next to a large area that was covered in large boxes that people *lived in*. I'd never seen such a thing. A guy pulled up in a pickup with a camper shell. In the pickup bed, there was donated food that he called "obligatory slop." Nothing as nice as a roast or even hamburger meat was offered. It was all cheap food, prepared in the cheapest way possible without much seasoning. The people who made and donated this food would never have served it to their family or friends. Never. No way.

I'll never forget the taste of Obligatory Slop. The homeless lined up, and we lined up with them. We were grateful to have anything to eat and something cool to drink. We were tired, hot and hungry. We didn't smell any better than the homeless did. Never again will I take for granted that I can bathe, brush my teeth and put on clean clothes every day.

As for the Obligatory Slop, I now find joy in offering nicer meals to the sick, hurting and poor than I might have before that trip. I am ashamed that I have been such a snob at times, rather than lavishing God's love in the same expensive, extravagant, generous way that He does. *1 John 3* tells about how God *lavishes* His love on us. He doesn't hold anything back, does He? Nope, He pours all His goodness over us.

Yet, we offer God our leftovers and the least of what we have sometimes too, don't we? We offer something meager just to say we offered something, like we're pulling one over on God. Right.

We got to know these homeless people, as we saw pretty much the same ones at each mealtime and we'd sit and visit with them. One man, I'll call Henry, was a drug addict. He had left his wife and children in favor of a fix. He once held a lucrative job before he chose drugs over his family. He lost it all. Henry was a nice enough guy, and I told him that there was hope; that God loved Him; that he could be forgiven.

Later, it occurred to me that I was willing to offer all the benefits of Jesus to a complete stranger, but I wasn't willing to do that for my own brother, with whom I was not on good terms. That was a watershed moment in my life.

I was convicted to obey God and quit making excuses. He asks me to love my brother. Period.

I learned about loving someone past whatever differences we might have. I learned that we don't have to agree to be kind and to care about someone. I'm sincerely sorry that it took me so long to realize that. I'm thankful that Cory was willing to meet me where I was while I was meeting him where he was.

About ten years later, when our dad was sick and dying, it helped that Cory and I were able to work together. We were both on Team Jerry, and it was one of the most special times of my life. Once again, obeying God was ultimately the best solution.

Go figure.

If you haven't read the book "Same Kind of Different as Me" by Ron Hall and Denver Moore, I hope you will consider doing so. It opened my eyes further to the plight of the homeless and those who are suffering. God gives us many opportunities to love on "the least of these" in His Kingdom. Jesus said we would always have the poor with us, and he admonished us to not look at the outward appearance, but rather the heart. In fact, I am humbled by the generosity of those who have little. In my experience over the past few years, they are more willing to share what they have, while I have, at times, been busy offering Obligatory Slop.

Besides our three summer trips to The Fortress, we have had several opportunities to share with the homeless and nearly homeless. It can be messy to love on those who don't have access to a bath and fresh, clean clothes each day. It is also eye-opening.

A few years ago, our daughter and her husband befriended a homeless man. They met him on the street corner near their church, selling newspapers on Sundays. They got to know him and would invite him over for dinner once a month or so. A couple of years later, we got to meet this man, I'll call Fred, who was in his late 50's. Our son-in-love, Matt, coached us on how to make conversation with Fred: don't ask a lot of questions and don't assume anything. It was awkward at first, but when Ashley and Matt moved away, Steve and I continued our friendship with Fred. He's a good guy with a remarkable heart to care for others, and who spends his time reading his Bible. He works a little, but his needs are small. He is no longer homeless. He opens his heart and his apartment to those who need to see Jesus.

He is philosophical about his time as a homeless man. He says he wouldn't know the Bible like he does if he had been working to pay the rent and maintain a home. He also says it helped him to genuinely love his fellow man. He doesn't offer Obligatory Slop.

I don't know about you, but that convicts me. Fred has learned to love everyone. Always. Even the ones who would make some of us squirm.

What would happen if we started to look for ways to connect with everyone we meet? What if we prayed for God to send those into our path that we can love and then ask Him to show us how to love them?

WooHoo! Hang on.

One of my kids has said that I need a t-shirt that reads, "Y'all need Jesus!" (I'll take that in hot pink, please.) The older I get, the more I internalize that truth. Nothing else matters but Him. I'm still trying to see folks through His eyes. It takes a bit of practice.

Actually, it takes quite a bit of practice for this former Obligatory Slop slinger.

What's Up With the
Words Written in Red?

In *John 13:34-35*, Jesus is talking - *"A new command I give you: Love one another. As I have loved you, so you must love one another. By this everyone will know that you are my disciples if you love one another."*

Right after Jesus washed His disciples' feet in *John 13*, we move right into *John 14*. If you ever wonder if love is important, read these two chapters. In them, we find out how to love Jesus: Obey Him.

So, what all does He ask of us?
To love the Lord, our God with all our heart and with all our soul and with all our strength and with all our mind.
To love our neighbor and ourselves.
To love our enemy and pray for those who persecute us.
To love one another.
To do unto others as we would have them do to us.
To forgive.

Those words are written in red in my Bible. Jesus said them. If we love and forgive, then that's how He knows we love Him!

A few of His words written in red:
John 14:15 *"If you love me, keep my commands.*
John 14: 21 *Whoever has my commands and keeps them is the one who loves me. The one who loves me will be loved by my Father, and I too will love them and show myself to them."*
John 14: 23 *Jesus replied, "Anyone who loves me will obey my teaching. My Father will love them, and we will come to them and make our home with them.*

Wow! We are loved by the Father; Jesus will show Himself to us, and The Father and Son will come and make their home with us.

This is so great! Love folks. Pray for folks. Forgive folks. I can do that.

Ok, it's not always easy, but if God asks us to do something, I have to believe it is entirely possible.

It's all about seeking that higher ground. Sometimes, that means taking the high road and choosing to ignore the low, hateful things, like unforgiveness and gossip. You see, I am certain that this life isn't about me. It's about God. Why am I here? To bring honor and glory to Him. I serve at the pleasure of The King. The King doesn't serve at the pleasure of Carrie. While He does love us enough to give His Son as a sacrifice for our sins, rescuing us from eternal death, He is not our *Genie in a bottle*. I've searched the Word and cannot find anywhere that it says that God wants us to be happy and comfortable. He wants us to love, to obey, to rejoice, to trust Him.

If He's all that matters, why do we fill our lives with so much other stuff? There is a God-shaped spot in you that the world will *never* satisfy.

Do we hunger for God? I contend that we do not, because we are constantly nibbling at the table the world has set for us. We are so comfortable. Do we pray to be uncomfortable? I don't. But, the Lord wants us to trust Him, whatever happens.

God's love for us is crazy unexplainable, crazy unwarranted, crazy unending and crazy generous. The world expects us to be selfish, unforgiving and hateful. When we show His love in hard circumstances, they wonder if we're crazy. Yes. Yes, we are!

It's all the more harmful when those of us who are 'churched' are the harsh, back-stabbing, gossips. My dear reader, please remember that the Almighty can work on any heart to help it get past any roadblock. When He gives us a commandment, the Creator of the Universe can help us make it happen. If we trust Him with it, He will make it beautiful. I promise.

Never mind that...*He promised.*

That sentence from many years ago is handy in many areas of life. "I love him more than I hate _____" even works when we're trying to bridge gaps in relationships with our family and friends. Think about someone that you've had a disagreement with (let me just jump on out on a limb and guess that it didn't take you long to picture someone).

Do you love them more than you hate what they did or said? Most of us might say, "Yes."

But, if the hurt is particularly fresh or profound, your answer may be "No."

Then, maybe we can ask ourselves if we love Jesus more than we hate whatever that person said or did. That usually gets to the very foundation of the issue because I love Jesus with all that I am. And I remind myself then that Jesus loves that other person just like He loves me.

That is a big ol' slice of humble pie, isn't it?

So, now apply that logic to loving everybody. Yes, everybody.
I love them more than I hate how they look.
I love them more than I hate how they smell.
I love them more than I hate their coarse language.
I love them more than I hate their political views.
I love them more than I hate their orange Mohawk.
I love them more than I hate their piercings and tattoos.
I love them more than I hate how uncomfortable I feel.
I love them more than...anything.

Now, we're getting somewhere, aren't we?

We never see others more clearly than when we look at them as Jesus looks at them, and that's with love – absolute and unconditional love. When we've adjusted our *hearts,* our *eyes* can see as Jesus sees.

Mahatma Gandhi said, "Be the change you wish to see in the world."

So, what happens if we become the change we wish to see in the world?

What happens if we are in line at the grocery store, and we see a mom with a kid who is running wild? Do we look at her with contempt? Or, do we go over to her and *find some way to encourage her*?

What happens if we're driving and someone cuts us off? Do we shake our fist and holler? Or do we *say a prayer* that they safely get where they're going?

When someone is wearing something that isn't modest, do we glare at them with disdain? Or do we *smile and tell them "I hope you have a great day!"*

People are used to getting a judging, holier-than-thou attitude. What happens if every single person you see gets a smile from you? Maybe a compliment? Maybe a "God bless you!"?

Yeah, how about that? Let's do that!

I'll never be closer to His will than when I love on His children. All of them.

Washing His Feet With My Tears

It took being knocked to my knees for me to fully understand just how judgmental and arrogant I had been.

Several years ago, we had the failed business and its accompanying debt, adult kids who were not behaving as we had hoped, and a son headed to Iraq for the second time. I was emotionally beaten down. In late May, we found out we were going to be grandparents by our older daughter, Ashley, and her husband, Matt. Things were looking up. We had heard that grandkids were pretty dandy, and we figured that we could use some *dandy* in our lives!

Then, one early evening in late June, our younger son, Jonathan, came to the house and plopped down on one of the kitchen barstools while Steve and I were getting ready for supper. I noticed that he looked nervous. He didn't make us wait long, as he bluntly said, "Lindsey's pregnant."

I gotta tell you, I smiled because...well, what else was I gonna do...on the outside?

Yes, my mind was reeling, and I was thinking "WHAT?!" I was stunned. I wanted to cry, but I also wanted to put on a confident face because he was noticeably scared. It was as if this was one of my life's pivotal moments and if I made a mistake here, everything could be won or lost with my son. I wasn't willing to lose. This was not what I wanted for him or our family, but it is precisely what we had to work with at that split-second.

All the parental sex talk conversations we'd had with him during his twenty-three years of breathing were running through my mind, and I figure they were running through his mind, too. I was angry and upset, but I just couldn't bring myself to say a single cross word to him.

Steve told him, "I know you can't see it now, but everything will be ok", and then Steve prayed as the three of us held hands. (Did I pick the greatest man on this planet to be the father of my children, or what?!)

The young couple had been dating for about two years. But, there was a problem: They had broken up almost a month before finding out they were pregnant. There was some bickering and lots of hurt feelings, but even more, there was fear of the unknown. She comes from a loving Christian home. Our son comes from a loving Christian home. Surely, we didn't need to be afraid. But, we were.

I was.

I cried. I cried for my child. I cried for our family. I cried for her. I cried for her family. All the hopes and dreams we had for our son were compromised and uncertain because now, he was going to be a daddy. Jonathan and Lindsey's decisions were all theirs to make, and I had to sit back, watch, keep my mouth shut and live with their consequences. (Easy for a control freak? Ummm, NO.)

After I had caught my breath, I remember just waving off the lies the world was (loudly and persistently) whispering in my ear. I stepped out in faith and did what Jesus asks me to do: I loved all of them. I loved my son. I loved Lindsey. I loved her parents. Through the tears, I just put one foot in front of the other, pasted on a smile and pressed forward, trusting and hoping.

We had family and friends who stood by us. God bless them for all the *heck* they probably took for it. We also had friends who told us they couldn't, in good conscience, condone an unwed pregnancy. Folks meant well when they counseled Steve and me to advise the young couple to get married or to not get married or to place the baby for adoption. Everyone had an opinion, and they thought we'd want to hear it.

It was such a painful time for every one of us on the front line of that battle. Unless you've been there, you can't imagine how much gets said that shouldn't have been said and how much goes unsaid that probably should have been said. It's like I was a giant raw wound and someone was frequently walking by and tossing in a handful of salt.

Being the mom of the daddy is harder than I was prepared to face. I have a friend who is the mom of the mommy and she got it worse than I did. It breaks my heart that we are the good church folks who claim to value the sanctity of life, but we sure do throw stones when it comes to a pregnancy before a wedding. We don't want to seem like we approve of premarital sex, so we just look down our noses and shake our heads, as if to say "you should've been a better parent."

Like I wasn't reviewing my mothering career and trying to see where I went wrong. Thanks. Thanks for pointing out how perfect your children are. I'm sure they haven't made any mistakes. Yeah, it's all me. I coulda, shoulda, woulda done something differently.

But, this was *our son* and *our grandbaby*. You don't know how you'll react until it happens to you and those you love most. You'd do anything to love them through it. Of course, we want our kids to be married and have jobs before they choose to start a family. But, life happens, and we need to realize that children who are terrified of their parents' reaction to a baby before a wedding are the very ones who don't make the best choices in a crisis.

When Lindsey found out she was going to have a baby, she went to Parkridge Pregnancy Center, where she received sound counsel, hope, and some prenatal vitamins.

(If you have a chance to donate to a crisis pregnancy center that focuses on Life and Hope, please send them lots of money! The young ladies who find themselves in an unplanned situation need a safe place to get care, helpful information, and reassurance. It's not the end of the world, but it sure feels like it to these gals. Thank you for caring.)

Later that year, Ashley and Matt gave us our first beautiful granddaughter, and then four days later, Jonathan and Lindsey gave us our first handsome grandson. We have a big family, and I like to think that God gave us two babies at one time because we'd have worn one out with all the rocking and cuddling we did.

Stephen and I say that grandbabies are better than air! No, really. They are just *so marvelous*. You have this little bundle of precious sweetness that reminds you of all that is right in the world. You get to watch your babies love on their babies. You get to witness unconditional love from every angle.

Lindsey is precious to me. She and Jonathan tried to make it work, to no avail. She got married when the baby was almost two years old, and it wasn't to our son. Thankfully, her husband is a remarkable man who loves our grandson, which is an answered prayer of this Grammie.

We now have two more granddaughters and three more grandsons, with another one on the way. We chose to be Grammie and Papa to our grandson's brothers because we believe that God isn't in the business of subtracting and dividing, but of adding and multiplying, especially when love is a crystal-clear commandment. What an example it is to our children and grandchildren that we don't bicker and make snide remarks, but we are kind to one another, and we pray for each other.

It's important to share with you the blessings that have come into our lives because we are choosing to love the mother of our grandson. I made her a promise that will last till my dying day: I love her, and I will always pray for God's best in her life. I realize that not one thing matters but that Jonathan, Lindsey, and their child get to Heaven. I refuse to let the devil lie to me and tell me to be petty and hateful. I am old enough and smart enough to know that child only wins if he sees love.

Lindsey's parents are fun, loving and fun-loving people who have become our friends. Together, we decided that, as their parents, we were going to set the best possible example. We've committed to love each other's child, as though they were our own. That means, when they are un-loveable (like we all are sometimes), we still love them and encourage them. We are choosing to love each other like we want to be loved.

It is beyond my wildest dreams to see how powerful that continues to be! God is always faithful and keeps His promises. When it comes time for birthday parties, ball games or other special occasions, all our families come together to celebrate a life. A life! I'm talking about our family, her family and her husband's family. It is such a blessing. There's a lot to celebrate!

Lindsey has thanked our family for always including her as a part of our family. She said, "You make me feel so loved." All of our grandbabies call her Aunt Lindsey, and her husband is Uncle Riley. They deserve no less. I am overcome when I think how bad this relationship could be if I had listened to the evil one. Praise God for showing us how to love!

Jonathan, Lindsey, and Riley have forged a unique relationship of respect and purpose with the best interest of all these children in mind. It warms my heart to see Jonathan loving on his son's brothers. In fact, he often takes all three boys, and they have a blast together.

Last Christmas found unlikely dinner companions, by the world's standard, sitting down together and carrying on companionable conversation. All the grands were wearing matching jammies for a requisite family photo shoot and a good time was had by all.

Who does that? Think about that from the points of view of Jonathan, Lindsey, and Riley. Again, I ask: Who does that?

I know the answer and so do you: someone who knows about the tremendous power of unconditional love; someone who has seen Heaven.

So, let's go back to that part where I was reviewing my mothering career and trying to see where I went wrong. Let me just say, I don't think I did go wrong. Steve and I raised

Jonathan to become an amazing daddy. I couldn't be more proud of the man he is.

The quote from Aristotle has never been truer: *"The whole is greater than the sum of its parts."*

As I re-read and re-live this story for the umpteenth time, copious, thankful tears still flow. I know without a doubt that He is Lord. What a mighty God we serve!

I have grieved the loss of Lindsey as my daughter-in-law, though she and Jonathan were never married. While I prayed that God would do as He saw fit, I was kind of hoping He'd see fit to have them work it out and be married forever. That was not to be, and I was terribly disappointed. And by *terribly disappointed*, I mean I cried for weeks and months. However, my husband reminds me that we got *just what we prayed for*: a healthy child living in a loving home. Blessed be the Name of the Lord!

My eyes started leaking just a little bit when I told Jonathan that I'd be sharing this part of my story, but that I wanted him to approve what would be written, since it's his story, too. He said, "Tell it. It happened." He was smiling. When I think about it, he has a lot to smile about, and Steve was right – everything is okay.

The tears I cry today are of happiness, not of loss. There is much joy in our family and, Lord willing, there is much more jubilation to come. From the time our children were born, I've prayed for their future spouses. I'm still praying and am confident that God will send Miss Wonderful his way. What an exciting time that will be!

Maybe you have a similar circumstance. It's never too late to start loving others as Christ loves us. It's not easy to step outside of the great anger or debilitating fear.

I know. I know.

I remember telling God, "I don't trust those two to make good choices, but You...You I trust. Please fix this." It was much easier to let God have my problems when I honestly trusted Him. He loves my family more than I do. What a thought.

I kneel at the Cross of the One who loves us most of all and I'll humbly shed enough tears to wash His precious feet. Thank you, Jesus!

and unrepentant that God will send Miss Woolstulp his
was what an exciting time that would ...

Maybe you have a similar dream ... they ... us ... but
to start by ... others as Christ loves us ...
outside of the great anger or debt ...

I know, I know ...

I remember telling God "I don't ...
good choices, but you know I think I'm ...
much easier to let God have my problems ...
trusted Him, He loves me Lanie ...
thought.

I knelt at the Cross of the Dove ...
I humbly shed tears ... team ... with Him ...
Thank you Jesus.

128

Time Out in a 32' Travel Trailer

You are in God's sight and you have been since the moment you came to be. You can't run or hide or change how He feels about you. You are precious to Him!

I'm sad to share with you that there were *years* that I made a choice to avoid God, to not be all that He made me to be. Then, thankfully, came the time that I realized that I was just no good at running it myself, so I asked God to take control of my life. Like the writer of Psalm and Jonah, I learned that I couldn't hide from God. Like them, I tried, and I failed.

Search me, God, and know my heart; test me and know my anxious thoughts. See if there is any offensive way in me, and lead me in the way everlasting.
-- Psalm 139:23-24

Intellectually, we know that we need to surrender to God's will in our lives, but in practice, we yank the controls back or maybe we're sly, and we just tell ourselves that we might be better at knowing what we need in our lives...than our *Creator*.

In 2008, I read Beverly Johnson's book, "Stick a Geranium in Your Hat and Be Happy." In it, she talks about her family life. She had some tough things happen to the point that she was fed up and wanted to kill herself. Before the fateful moment, she realized that she'd been giving the problems to God, then taking them back. Finally, she decided to give it all to God and be done with it. She said something along the lines of "Whatever, Lord. Whatever."

At that time, Josh was in Iraq for his second tour. To put it mildly, I was anxious for his well-being. One morning, he called to let us know his new mailing address as his unit had moved to a more dangerous location. As moms do, I stuffed it down until I could get off the phone. I had to get ready for work, but I spent a good bit of extra time in the shower that morning, sobbing from the depths of my soul, and beseeching God's favor and protection for my child.

Our youngest, Shannel, was planning a wedding, so I was working hard to pay for everything. I had a new management job in an industry in which I had no experience, so I was feeling inadequate. We were still chipping away at the debt from our failed business, and I was taking phone calls from bill collectors daily.

It's true when you're flat on your back in despair, there's no place to look but up. I finally got brave enough to pray, "Whatever, Lord. Whatever. Josh is yours. Ashley is yours.

Jonathan is yours. Shannel is yours. Whatever happens, Lord, I am yours."

Whatever happens. Whatever.

That's when things began to change for me. The difference was fairly dramatic. Bad things didn't stop happening. I just trusted God for deliverance...and peace settled on me. Our car still broke down. The toilet still overflowed. People I love still died. Life continued to occur as *Ecclesiastes* promised it would. What did change was where I placed my confidence. Being a child of the King holds a promise that we never have to face the hard times alone.

In 2010, a couple of my close friends had life-changing illnesses. One was about sixty, and she had a stroke. She is doing well now, but is unable to work anymore, so she had to sell her half of a business that she started and had to file for permanent disability. The other was a mom of two teenagers, and she was diagnosed with Stage 4 Leukemia. Her cancer is in remission following a bone marrow transplant a few years ago.

Watching these two ladies have to make decisions they never thought they'd have to make gave me an opportunity to stop and think about the moments I had left in my life. I asked myself, "You've been working for years for *someday*, when you'll slow down, write that book, take a gourmet cooking class, travel, enjoy life, relax and spend more time with family and friends...so what if *some day* doesn't come?

What about now?" I knew that none of us are promised a tomorrow, but we do have today. We have now.

That led me to do some intense soul-searching.

We had built our dream home on an acre lot in a peaceful neighborhood outside the city limits. There were no streetlights, so we could sit outside in the evenings and see the stars and listen to nature. We loved the location and our neighbors. The house and yard were perfect for parties, so we had a bunch of them.

When our kids were there to help with the cleaning, mowing, and upkeep, it was the ideal place for us. When our offspring left home to start their own lives, Mr. B and I decided that we didn't like doing all that work ourselves. Seriously, we had a bunch of kids because we didn't want to clean our own house or mow our own yard (just kidding...kind of). We already worked hard to afford the house, then we had to come home and put in several hours of work each week to keep it looking like we wanted it to. After our neighbor had her stroke and my friend was diagnosed with cancer, we began to wonder, "If we don't *carpe diem* now, then when?"

We sold that lovely home and moved into a 32-foot travel trailer that we parked in our son's driveway. We needed time to decide where we wanted to live next, so we planted ourselves in Time Out and gave ourselves some breathing room.

I learned a few things while living in that 32' travel trailer:

-I don't need much to run a house and make a home. If you can't find it in here, you don't need it...probably.

-I had too much stuff before. It was nice to look at, but not so much fun to dust.

-I don't need a closet full of clothes.

-The wind is loud.

-Rain is loud.

-Get over it. Pride is deceptive. Your true friends don't care what you have. It's more important to live within, or better yet, to live beneath your income. We are not to lay up treasures for ourselves here, but rather in Heaven. Give more away than you keep. As long as we hold tightly to our blessings, we cannot realize the pure joy that comes from opening our hands and letting our temporary possessions be just that, temporary.

-Share the space and find a way to get along.

-Only one person at a time can get ready in a hurry.

-We really do spin and toil.

-I don't like the anxiety that comes from needing every penny we have.

-They are God's pennies anyway.

-He is the Lord of my life. The sooner I submit to Him and turn my day over to Him, the sooner I can grasp the peace and joy He has for me. Whether I choose to live within His will or not, life is full of trials: the washer leaks, the car quits, and grandma dies. I can't control any of it. Any. Of. It.

-Who really needs 5 slotted spoons, 12 large knives, 2 peelers, 6 spatulas, 5 pitchers and 57 bowls?

-I have too many of everything!

-I miss having parties.
-We really like each other's company, which is a good thing because that's about all that can live in here.

People asked us if the walls closed in and we needed some space. No, it didn't. If it were just the two of us, we would have been perfectly content, but we love having our babies and their babies around, as well as our families and our friends. So, nine months later, we bought another, much smaller, home with a little front yard and a delightful cement pond in the back yard. We moved into it with a new attitude about people, things and our time here on earth.

During the time that we lived in the travel trailer, three of our friends died. Each death was unexpected, so there was no time for goodbyes or preparation. This was just all the more reason to make every minute count. We aren't promised tomorrow, so we chose to live life with abandon.

I ran across this poem several years ago, and it spoke to my heart about joyfully living in the present and not wishing away the once-in-a-lifetime occasions that we have each day.

Dance Like No One is Watching
We convince ourselves that life will be better after we get married, have a baby, then another.
Then we are frustrated that the kids aren't old enough and we'll be more content when they are.
After that, we're frustrated that we have teenagers to deal with. We will certainly be happy when they are out of that

stage. We tell ourselves that our life will be complete when our spouse gets his or her act together, when we get a nicer car, are able to go on a nice vacation,
or when we retire.
The truth is, there's no better time to be happy than right now. If not now, when? Your life will always be filled with challenges. It's best to admit this to yourself and decide to be happy anyway. Happiness is the way. So, treasure every moment that you have and treasure it more because you shared it with someone special, special enough to spend your time with...and remember that time waits for no one.

So, stop waiting
--until your car or home is paid off
--until you get a new car or home
--until your kids leave the house
--until you go back to school
--until you lose ten pounds
--until you gain ten pounds
--until you finish school
--until you get married
--until you have kids
--until you retire
--until summer
--until spring
--until winter
--until fall
--until you die

There is no better time than RIGHT NOW to be happy.

Happiness is a JOURNEY, not a destination.
So -- work like you don't need money,
Love like you've never been hurt,
And dance like no one's watching.
--Author Unknown

I don't know your story, but I do know that time passes in the same manner for all of us. We all have twenty-four hours in our day and it's up to us to decide how to invest ourselves into the passing moments. Maybe you are still in school. Maybe you have a career. Maybe you don't. Maybe you have a young family. Maybe you're single. Maybe you have an empty nest. Maybe you have aging parents who need you to care for them.

No matter our personal circumstances, let's both take a moment to gain perspective. If we didn't have a *home*, it wouldn't need to be cleaned or decorated. If we didn't have a *car*, a tire couldn't go flat. If we had no *children,* we wouldn't trip over toys, or have to attend a ballet, choir or sporting event, and there wouldn't be piles of laundry. If we had no *spouse*, we wouldn't have to cook or share a bed. If our *parents* were already in Heaven, we wouldn't have to take them to countless doctor appointments or remind them of our name or listen to the same goofy stories one more time. ...or maybe, we could be thankful for our *homes, cars, children, spouse, parents,* as well as our leaky faucets, piles of mending and goofy old stories.

And now, from the department of
When am I Gonna Learn...

It was the week of Thanksgiving in 2010. I'd been begging God for several things for weeks, months, years. I was bone-weary. It was the week that our grandson's mom was marrying a man who was not my son. I was grieving the loss of her as my daughter-in-law and for the three of them to be a family. We were still wading through the debt. It was my busiest season at work, and I saw no relief coming on any front.

I saw people on Facebook posting things they were thankful for every day in November. Quite frankly, it annoyed me to see the posts. That sounds awful, but it's the truth. I was wondering, "Why me?" and still hosting a daily, never-ending pity party. A particular scripture hit me over and over until I finally paid attention.

Do not be anxious about anything, but in every situation, by prayer and petition, with thanksgiving, present your requests to God. – Philippians 4:6

I *was* anxious about everything. I *wasn't* praying, it was more like begging, and I didn't remember to be thankful for the blessings I already had. So, I decided to shake things up a bit and for that one week, I wouldn't ask God for anything. I'd just be thankful.

Oh, my dear goodness...*peace and joy washed over my soul* more and more as the week progressed. I became less anxious. I even smiled...and laughed! I did like the song says, I counted my blessings, naming them one by one and I *was* surprised at what the Lord had done in my life. I was suddenly thankful for all those years of cleaning toilets, doing laundry, buying groceries, attending school functions and sporting events because that meant I had raised a beautiful family and made some wonderful memories. I had *lived*!

I believe that the Holy Spirit opened my eyes to see outside my pain, disappointment, fear, and despair. I decided to continue to be thankful. Little by little, the things I'd been begging for, came to pass. Whether the answer was Yes, No or Later, I didn't care, I was just thankful. And having a grateful spirit changed me from the inside out.

If you are spinning and toiling today, please take a minute to give thanks for your blessings (I guarantee they outnumber your troubles). Stand up straight and choose to live a life of purpose. Share a kind word. Forgive and work on forgetting. Be real. Spend time with those who matter to you.

When necessary, put yourself in Time Out.

Handy Dandy Instructions for Cheerful Giving

Being an adult is overwhelming. Sometimes, the money runs out before the month does. It can be a challenge to live from paycheck to paycheck. It takes commitment (and acting like a grown- up) to take care of our responsibilities. I've been there many, many times. I remember being envious of those who seemed to have plenty of money. I would later learn that it was because they were good stewards.

When I was a young married woman, our friends made a point of giving their contribution at church before they paid any of their monthly bills. I couldn't imagine taking out for God first when there wasn't enough to pay all the bills in the first place, and I told them so. They said, "Trust God. He will take care of you if you honor Him." I was skeptical and immature, so I kept merrily skipping down the path of destruction and poverty.

The Old Testament tells us that God required a tithe, or tenth, be given to Him. He didn't want the leftovers, He asked that the best grain and animals be set aside for Him.

In the New Testament, we don't see the actual word *tithe*, but there is much talk of giving. One example is in *2 Corinthians 9:6-15*, where it tells us that God loves a cheerful giver and that our being generous in sharing causes others to thank God. I hope you'll read that passage and consider it.

That particular story reminds me of a time in about 1999 when we were, as usual, broke. During a counseling session, we were asked if we were giving at church. We tried to get technical so we could hang on to every possible penny, and we asked, "Are we supposed to give out of our gross or our net income?" His answer? "Do you want God to bless you out of the gross or the net?"

Ouch!

Who wouldn't rather be blessed out of the gross than the net? Yet, I was still immature and found ways to be deceitful. Like I was fooling God. Oh, my stars!

We were learning, but our education wasn't complete until many years later when we got serious about getting out of debt. We took a class and made a concerted effort to be better stewards. The first lesson...and I do mean the *first* lesson... was on giving to God.

Giving? But, we don't have enough money as it is!
Give.
But, we can be out of debt faster if we don't give.
Give.

From that point, we started telling ourselves that we were good stewards. We made decisions based on the fact that we were good stewards. We began to give because we were good stewards. We thanked God because He gave us something to steward.

When we told ourselves we were broke, we were broke. When we told ourselves we weren't good money managers, we weren't good money managers. When we made the smallest of efforts to *be* more, then we *were* more. Funny how that works, huh?

Are you feeling your chest tighten and your breathing quicken as the panic creeps over you? Stop. Please. Take a deep breath. Bear with me, please.

The story of the widow's mite in *Mark 12* tells of the wealthy folks throwing large amounts of money into the temple treasury while a poor widow came and put in two very small copper coins, worth only a fraction of a penny. *Jesus saw this and said "I tell you the truth, this poor widow has put more into the treasury than all the others. They gave out of their wealth; but she, out of her poverty, put in everything – all she had to live on."*

It doesn't explicitly say, but if Jesus took the time to note her generosity and it was in line with what He was asking, do you think maybe He made sure that she didn't go hungry?

Malachi 3 tells the story where God asked the Israelites why they were robbing Him. *They asked, "How do we rob you?" He replied, "In tithes and offerings....Test me in this and see if I will not throw open the floodgates of Heaven and pour out so much blessing that you will not have room enough for it."*

There are so many examples where God shows us that if we are faithful to Him, He will protect us. I'm not preaching a Gospel of Prosperity. I'm preaching the Gospel of Jesus that asks us to trust and obey. Will bad things happen? Yes, they will. The car will break down, someone will be laid off, or the electricity might get turned off. Life will continue as it always has.

The hard part for me was that we put ourselves in some pretty bad situations because of naïve choices we made. So, when the electricity was cut off, it was because we had not wisely managed what money we did have. I could give many examples of mismanagement, but the point is that Steve and I were selfish and had no regard to putting God first.

Thanks to the generous example of God, we have learned what it means to give and to be generous. A few times, we've tried to out-give God, and we just can't do it. When we give out of our comfort and prosperity, it's good, but when we dig deep and give till it hurts, God does His best work in us.

I wonder if that's why the word *tithe* isn't in the New Testament. The legalistic rule-followers may have been dutifully giving a tenth of their first fruits, but maybe their rigid hearts were not cheerful nor were their motives pure (cue Ananias and Sapphira).

In the New Testament, we have freedom from the law. We are free to give Him everything. There are no rules, so that leaves lots of room for unwavering love to be our guide for extravagant giving.

My favorite times are when He unexpectedly asks me to do something for someone else. One day, while I visiting with one of our Aflac policyholders at her place of employment, she requested prayer because her husband was using their grocery money for liquor to the point that she didn't have enough for food the week of Thanksgiving. She and I prayed right then and there. As I was leaving the building, I had an overwhelming sense that she needed the money that was in my pocket.

I must tell you three things. Number one, I am not talking about a quiet voice inside saying, "Carrie, you can give her the money you have in your pocket." No. I'm talking about feeling a surge of awareness because my heart started racing, and I couldn't keep walking away. Literally, *couldn't keep walking away.*

Number two, I'm the kind of gal that owns a few pairs of nice slacks for work, but only one pair with pockets. I had them on that day.

Number three, I never carry cash in my slacks during a work day. We have a business checking account, so I might carry my debit card to pay for a business lunch, but never do I carry cash.

However, somehow that day, I had worn the right slacks, and the right circumstances led me to have cash in my pocket. Draw your own conclusions, but I *know* why all those things came together that day: one of God's children needed His help, and He used one of His children to help another one of His children.

This is not about me or the cash, so please don't stop at the surface of this story. It's about listening to Him, knowing that when I feel a nudge or hear a voice or have a power surge that turns me around in my tracks, it's Him. I'm not sure why it shocked me that after asking Him to work in my life, He did just that. When I followed the urging, my friend was astonished because her prayers were heard, and we were both in tears because we knew for certain that we were in the holy presence of God.

In *Acts 2:38*, Peter tells the crowd, *"Repent and be baptized, every one of you, in the name of Jesus Christ for the forgiveness of your sins. And you will receive the gift of the Holy Spirit."*

We can have that powerful Spirit within us. If one of God's children asks Him for help, maybe it'll be me that He sends on the rescue mission. This street has two-way traffic, so sometimes we give and sometimes, we receive. We have been the grateful recipients of His rescue missions when others have heard His voice.

Right now, if you have more month than money, please study the passages mentioned here and make a commitment to give to God out of your first fruits. He will not let you go hungry, and He will provide for your needs. Don't worry (*Matthew 6:25-34*).

Please don't be tempted, as I was, to be evasive and say, "But I give God my time and I give Him my thanks for all He blesses me with." That's a start, but He asks for all of it, our complete and unconditional surrender: our day, our checking account, our future, our family...all of it. He wants all of it. It's His anyway, isn't it? God doesn't need our money. He needs us.

"Which of you, if your son asks for bread, will give him a stone? Or if he asks for a fish, will give him a snake? If you then, though you are evil, know how to give good gifts to your children, how much more will your Father in Heaven give good gifts to those who ask Him!" -- Matthew 7:9-11

Please note, that isn't a question, it's an emphatic statement written in bright red letters in my Bible. I love that!

There is so much pain in this world. Those who don't know Him, don't understand His ways. Step on out there and give, give, give like He does. You'll be surprised how it will cheer you up.

See how I tied this whole chapter up with a big fancy bow?
Be a cheerful giver!

Pray. Love. Forgive.

Have you heard the story of Jesus and the woman caught in adultery?

The teachers of the law and the Pharisees brought in the woman, made her stand before the group and said to Jesus, "Teacher, this woman was caught in the act of adultery. In the Law, Moses commanded us to stone such women. Now, what do you say?" They were trying to trap him to have an excuse to accuse him. But Jesus bent down and started to write on the ground with his finger. When they kept on questioning Him, he straightened up and said to them "If any of you is without sin, let him be the first to throw a stone at her." John 8:3-7

Aren't these some of the most powerful words in scripture? If any of us is without sin, we can throw the first stone and feel justified and righteous. Right?

All of us have lived a life that is riddled with pain and hurt. We've been on the receiving end and let's be honest, the giving end, too. Let's just cut to the chase and realize that

147

we intend to forgive, *but*...do you realize what he did? Do you know what she said?

Lord's Prayer – *Luke 11* - One day Jesus was praying in a certain place. When he finished, one of his disciples said to him, *"Lord, teach us to pray, just as John taught his disciples." Jesus said to them, "When you pray, say: "'Father, hallowed be your name, your kingdom come. Give us each day our daily bread. Forgive us our sins, for we also forgive everyone who sins against us. And lead us not into temptation.'"*

"So I say to you: Ask and it will be given to you; seek and you will find; knock and the door will be opened to you. For everyone who asks receives; the one who seeks finds; and to the one who knocks, the door will be opened.

Visualize with me for a few moments, please. When we surrender our lives to God, what happens? We bring our burdens and hand them over to Jesus: our pain, our weariness, our selfishness. That's really what our sin is...our putting ourselves above all else. All sin has its root in selfishness. We stand there in the shadow of the King of Kings as His body hangs on the Cross. We come to fully realize that His blood is dripping because of our sin. My sin.

As I look up, His eyes are full of forgiveness, love and hope. I bring my shame to Him, and He tells me that He loves me, that I need to go and sin no more.

Reluctantly, I turn from the Cross to walk away. I turn back and ask Him, "Are you sure I should go? I'm the reason you're dying. I did this to you."

I imagine that He'd tell me once more, "I love you. Go and sin no more." And all the while He knows I'm going to sin again, yet He's hopeful that I will be mindful of what I've seen. I walk away, relieved of that which had weighed me down. Free. Forgiven. Loved.

I've been given this amazing gift of forgiveness, and now it's time to do some forgiving. I've heard the sermons and the songs, and yet, I still hold on to my grudges. I let some one or some thing take up space in my head and heart, rent-free. I foolishly argue with the Lord about why I feel justified hanging on to my anger and bitterness. Maybe I can put the person or situation out of my life - out of sight, out of mind. But it doesn't work that way. The person or issue may be buried, but it won't truly go away until I deal with it and do some forgiving. It's not easy or comfortable, but it is necessary.

And when you stand praying, if you hold anything against anyone, forgive him, so that your Father in Heaven may forgive your sins. -- Matthew 11:25

Again, I want to be forgiven, just like we want love, mercy and grace, but I can't seem to give as good as I get.

In the book of *Acts*, Jesus tells his disciples that God is going to give them a gift. It's talking about Him giving us the gift of the Holy Spirit. When we obey God, the Spirit comes in all His power. He equips us. Why do we deny ourselves that gift by hanging on to old sins and hurts?

Oh, my stars. Why do I fight Him?

Buckle up, it's gonna be a bumpy ride

As I've mentioned, our parents divorced when I was fourteen and my brother, Cory, was thirteen. Both our parents were married to someone else within the year. It was a rough time for a couple of teenagers. We both struggled in different ways, and we didn't have a close relationship until these past few years. I'm thankful that we found our way back to each other.

One of the things that drew us back together was the illness and death of our dad the summer of 2013.

Before that Tuesday, February 19 at 4 pm, I'd have said that I was a forgiving person; that I had my spiritual house in order. But, the enemy is the Father of Lies and is full of deceit and evil. There is a reason the Bible tells us to be aware, be vigilant...because he is roaming to and fro, seeking whom he may devour.

My dad was losing his memory. He had been doing some disturbing and odd things for the past few years. He'd retired from farming and had gotten a couple of jobs, but wasn't able to hold them. With the ever-reliable 20/20 hindsight, I'm sure he wasn't mentally capable of doing the jobs. He was telling the same stories each time we'd visit.

He was making his sweet neighbors uncomfortable with some of his odd behaviors. It was progressively getting worse.

Since he had time on his hands, he drove around a great deal...like about 700 miles a week. Because he was a life-long farmer, he enjoyed driving all around the countryside, looking at the fields and the crops. The money he spent on gas was a sore point with his wife, my stepmother. His behavior, in general, was a sore point. She and I had had countless conversations about Daddy, his behavior and how to improve the situations it created. He was pushing every button she had, and I could tell she was at the end of her rope, so to speak. She called me that Tuesday afternoon and said that she just couldn't do it anymore. She had decided to divorce him.

Steve and I had just left an enrollment at one of our Aflac accounts when she called. We grabbed a burger for supper and headed to their house, about a forty-five-minute drive away. We sat in their living room and I asked if there was anything we could do to help them stay together. Daddy looked to her as she said that it was too late. She informed us that they were going to be friends and have an amicable divorce. He wordlessly nodded in agreement.

Can you imagine how it felt to sit and listen to these (and other) words? I couldn't challenge her or argue because it would ultimately hurt Daddy. The whole situation seemed so unbelievable.

(Several conversations occurred over the course of that next few weeks that I'm not ready to see in print, plus the innocents would most certainly get caught in the crossfire. And while it might be cathartic for me to get it all out in the open, that's not my mission here. Remember, I just want you to know that I'm human. I've done the best I could with the cards I was dealt. And this was an exceedingly atrocious hand. As I sit on the fence between telling it all and being wise, it is still quite challenging to discreetly describe how much pain was involved for my kids and me, not to mention Cory, his daughter and Daddy's siblings and their families.)

Nonetheless, his wife was ready to be done with his care, so in March, I met Daddy and his soon-to-be ex-wife at the bank, and we took care of all the accounts and legal documents to move him to my care. He was able to live alone and drive, but he didn't remember to pay bills, so I began to take care of those and to make sure he had money for groceries, gas and cigarettes. It was a complete life change for my husband and me.

I know that some folks, who are caregivers for their parents, have a really hard time with their siblings, due to differences of opinion concerning care or a million other things. Cory was so great! He said, "You're there. I'm not. Do whatever you need to and I'll back you up." I'll always be thankful for his attitude and his support.

If I thought that this second divorce was going to be easier than the first, I was in for a rude awakening. I had often called my parents' divorce "the gift that keeps on giving." Now, there was more heartache, more pain and more unrest, no matter which way I turned. When marriage vows talk about *till death parts us*, it is for real. Divorce is a death. There are all the same steps of grief when a marriage dies – denial/isolation, anger, bargaining, depression, and acceptance. I didn't do them all in order, but I did them all.

I felt a great responsibility to make sure that Daddy was safe and that his interests were protected. Everything I did was done with several sets of eyes watching me and as it ended up, I'm so glad I did because I'd have second-guessed myself later. I called Cory every time something happened or when a decision was made. Because Daddy was easy-going, he would agree with just about anything, and I refused to manipulate him. I asked others to witness or confirm statements and decisions.

Shannel needed back surgery during this time. She had a baby that she wouldn't be able to lift or carry for eight weeks, so I went to stay with her and the baby so her husband, Jacob, could keep working. They lived about nine hours away. I stayed with them until she was healthy enough to travel, about three weeks, then I brought Shannel and the baby home with me so I could get back to work, at least part-time. She still wasn't supposed to lift the baby for another five weeks, and I was adamant that she needed her full recovery time. Too much was at stake for her health. We came home on a Friday.

Dad's second divorce was final on that following Monday. We talked by phone daily. Shannel wanted to see him and show off her precious baby who had just turned one, so we went to see him the following Sunday to take him to lunch. He didn't eat because he didn't feel well. He didn't look well either. He said he had pulled a muscle the day before and that his stomach was bothering him. I asked if I could take him on to the doctor and he said, "No. I'll be fine." I called him later that afternoon, and he sounded better, so I decided I'd check back the next day.

My brother called me the next morning and said that he'd called Dad, but that Dad couldn't talk. I called and it sounded like Dad's mouth was full of cotton balls, so I figured that he'd had a stroke. I called a friend to go by there and wait with him while I headed that way at a rapid rate of speed. The friend got there and decided to call an ambulance.

By the end of that day, the surgeon had performed surgery to remove his ruptured appendix. He was critically ill as he was septic, was on a ventilator and had a feeding tube. It took about three weeks to regain his mind and sense of humor. He loved telling jokes and stories to his captive audience, the nurses and his visitors. When asked about this, he said, "I just want to make people happy." In the mornings, he would know where he was and could give very accurate information. By evening, he was confused and agitated. We had plenty of hours to visit, and when there was no audience, he would ask heartbreaking questions, to which I had disappointing answers.

In the middle of all this, Shannel still couldn't take care of her baby, so her older sister, Ashley, came from Virginia to help. We had a house full of kids and grandkids, which should have been fun, but I was distracted. I was either at the hospital, sleeping, or on my way back to the hospital.

What else can happen?
Funny you should ask...

Two weeks into the fun and games with Dad, Steve hurt his back and couldn't walk for a few days. The day after Steve got hurt, I got a call from Barton, my stepdad, that my mom had fallen and broken her arm. She was in a San Antonio emergency room, six hours away. Being the wonderful guy he is, he said he would take care of her, and they both wanted me to not worry.

Yeah, right.

Sometimes life can be overwhelming. That's how I felt as I sat there and wondered how to take my next breath. Wave after wave was crashing over me as I kept valiantly fighting to stand back up. I needed to see my momma. Daddy was back in ICU, after being in a regular room for a couple of days. I couldn't even cry because that would take more than I had in me at that moment. No doubt, this was sensory overload. Mom's cousin called and asked if I was ok. I replied, "Not even close." As I remember the desperation I felt, this quote comes to mind: *Lord, I'm drowning, and it's too late to learn to swim.*

155

My cousin, Beth, took care of overseeing Dad's care while I went to be with Mom for her surgery. Several folks had offered to go with me on this road trip, but I wanted to be alone with my thoughts. Both of my parents, my child and my husband were all hurt, and I was tired of talking and making decisions. I needed the time alone to cry and talk to myself. That's healthy, right? Momma's surgery went well, and there was peace in my spirit after I got to love on her.

Eight days later, Dad was moved from the hospital to a rehab hospital on his 70th birthday. He kept asking to go home, saying he felt fine, but we kept reminding him that he couldn't take care of himself just yet. I asked him to do the rehab and told him that we'd do everything to get him back home again. However, it was just too much for his mind and his body. His ten-inch long incision was still open and healing. When he would look down at his chest and stomach, you could see that it was devastating to him. It was devastating to me, as well. Everything would be different now for both of us.

On Father's Day evening, the nursing staff was telling me how he wasn't eating or drinking enough, so it fell to me to give Daddy a pep talk, "You know they are all telling me how you need to eat and drink more, but I'm not going to fight you on this. You do what you want. You *can* get better, so I will come every day and do every step of your rehab beside you, and I will fight for you to get back to where you were. But, if this is what you want (pointing to him lying in bed), I will fight for you, and they will not put another tube in you." He nodded and said, "Okay" in a flat voice.

He was dead within just a few hours.

I had gone home and was asleep when the charge nurse called about 1:15 am and said he was deteriorating. As Steve and I hurriedly got dressed and headed to the rehab hospital, it never crossed my mind that he was dying that night. However, when I saw him, I knew this was the very end. I was able to get Cory on the phone to talk to Daddy because I knew Cory couldn't possibly make it from Pampa in time.

From that very moment, all the anger I'd been stuffing down since February (and for thirty-four years) boiled over. I had been talking to his ex-wife all through the divorce process and as he was in the hospital because I was still trying to keep the peace. But once I knew it was the end of his life, I was not willing to share these last moments with her. The depth and breadth of my anger surprised me because I knew that he died of a broken heart, a broken body and a broken spirit.

I had released many hurts and misunderstandings over the course of thirty-four years to protect my relationship with my Dad after he and my mom divorced. I resigned myself to the fact that I'd have to *go along to get along*. It took many years, but as I matured, I grew weary of the burden of remembering all the past hurts, so I gave it all to God and decided to live a life of peace. To have it turn out as it did, was a genuine blessing for me because my dad, brother and I got to spend those precious last four weeks together, telling stories and loving on each other, singing songs and making his nurses and visitors laugh.

Daddy's mind was failing. He had many moments of complete clarity, but there were many moments where he would ask the same questions over and over again. While he could have been physically healthy again, he was never going to be better mentally. Without a doubt, it was a very painful time for him. I am convinced that he made up his mind to be done when I promised him that I'd let him go, rather than letting them put tubes in him to just prolong his being on Earth.

I praise our merciful God!

Now, what?
A life of bitterness and anger makes me feel self-righteous and justified...but I'm not. It's a sin, and I have to deal with that.

Forgive...no ifs, ands or buts from our Savior. Please think about those you find unforgivable. I know you have someone in mind; maybe more than *one* someone. He loves the person that hurt you as much as He loves you. *I know it's hard to lay aside the past.* Do it anyway. Jesus could have called legions of angels to pull Him from the Cross. He hung there anyway.

I am a sinner, in need of a Savior, in need of forgiveness. I have received forgiveness for some pretty awful things:

deceit, anger, pride and selfishness. My Lord has been hurt by my choices.

The Good News of Jesus is love. The only way He says that others will know that we are His is by how we love one another. Along with His asking us to love, He asks us to forgive.

BUT...did you not see what all just happened?

Yes, God surely did. He asks me to love and forgive anyway.

How can I withhold something that I have received? He forgave me, how can I not forgive others?

I'm not saying it is easy, but I choose the life He has for me. I surrender to His will in my life because I surely have made a mess of it on my own. Do I still have stirrings of bitterness over things that were done or said? You bet, but I truly rest in Him...and I grasp the forgiveness He has given me. I feel His loving arms and hear His gentle voice through His Word. He calls me to a life that will bear the fruit of His Spirit in it: love, joy, peace, patience, kindness, goodness, faithfulness, gentleness, and self-control.

Galatians 5 contains these verses- *You, my brothers and sisters, were called to be free. But do not use your freedom to indulge the flesh; rather, serve one another humbly in love. For the entire law is fulfilled in keeping this one command: "Love your neighbor as yourself." If you bite and devour each other, watch out, or you will be destroyed by each other. So I say, walk by the Spirit, and you will not gratify the desires of the flesh. For the flesh desires what is contrary to the Spirit, and the Spirit what is contrary to the flesh. They are in conflict with each other so that you are not to do whatever you want. But if you are led by the Spirit, you are not under the law. The acts of the flesh are obvious: sexual immorality, impurity, and debauchery; idolatry and witchcraft; hatred, discord, jealousy, fits of rage, selfish ambition, dissensions, factions, and envy; drunkenness, orgies, and the like. I warn you, as I did before, that those who live like this will not inherit the kingdom of God. But the fruit of the Spirit is love, joy, peace, patience, kindness, goodness, faithfulness, gentleness, and self-control.*

Pray. Love. Forgive.

There's a lesson in my story for many of us. If you are a child of divorce: pray, love and forgive both your parents. If you are divorced: pray, love and forgive your spouse and yourself. If you are a step-parent: pray and truly love your spouse's children. If you are estranged from your siblings: pray, love and forgive. If you are angry: pray, love and forgive. If you look in the mirror every day and are disgusted with yourself and what you have done: pray, love and forgive yourself. Today. Do it today.

James tells us in chapter 4: *What is your life? You are a mist that appears for a little while and then vanishes.*

Do it today. Love and forgive. Just do it. Today.

Psalm 103:12 – as far as sunrise is from sunset, He has separated us from our sins. (The Message)

Stop *remembering* what God has *forgotten.*

Don't listen to the evil one whispering in your ear ...*BUT* remember what she said...what he did...what you did...what you said...

I know that dark place where we live when we have a troubled spirit...when we are hurt, angry and embarrassed; when grief and pain guide our every waking thought. It's not pretty. It's lonely. It's dreadful. But God is there, and He asks us to trust Him and live in His light.

May the God of Hope, fill you with all joy and peace as you trust in Him so that you may overflow with Hope by the Power of the Holy Spirit. -- Romans 15:13

Just do it. Love and forgive. Grasp the *hope* that He has for you. Grasp the *joy* and the *peace* that He has for your life. Grasp the hands of your friends and family who care about you and will help you through the tough times. Hang on for dear life, because that is just what is at stake.

Life.

If I'd Known I Was Going to Live This Long, I Would've Taken Better Care of Myself

I have some unconventional opinions about dying and death. First of all, I'm ready. Right now. Jesus, bring a bus and come get all of us who love you so! Get me outta this place and take me Home. I want to see those pearly gates and walk those streets paved with gold. I long to walk by the river of the water of life and to see the tree of life. I have high expectations for the exultant singing and the bountiful banquet table.

(My momma hates to hear me say all that, which I completely understand, but it doesn't stop me from yearning for Heaven.)

I can appreciate that the Spirit lives within me and gives me each breath, so I'm not disrespecting that glorious gift. I'm just not scared, nor am I hanging on especially tight to this mortal coil. There are no illusions, as I admit to having more days behind me than in front of me. I am not a physical being living a brief spiritual life here on Earth. I am an eternal spiritual being, living a brief physical life on this Earth.
Yes, all that.

Gayle

In the summer of 1991, my husband's dad was diagnosed with advanced liver cancer. Gayle, along with his wife, Mary, asked all their adult kids to go with them to see the surgeon about available treatment options. The prognosis was grim. The combination of surgery and chemotherapy would only buy him six to twelve months of life. Gayle asked what his quality of life would be. The doctor said, "You'll be very sick."

Gayle looked around the examination room and into the eyes of each of his children and asked, "Will you be mad at me if I don't choose the surgery and chemo? If I don't want to fight it?" They all gave him their blessing, so he told the doctor that he didn't want to spend what time he had left being sick. Five weeks later, he was in hospice care. Seven weeks later, he was gone.

(I heartily recommend hospice! They were everything we needed as they cared for Gayle and for his family. They were invaluable to us those last few days he was alive - answering questions and supporting our various needs.)

During his last day and night, Gayle was no longer responsive. Just a few hours before he died, some of us were sitting on his bed. We started singing old hymns. Gayle was lying on his back with his knees drawn up. As we sang, he began rocking his knees back and forth in tempo with the music. I began to see that a person who is leaving this world, already has a foot in the next one. I'd never thought of the metamorphosis before that night. I was able to see the last breath leave his body as he crossed the river that we all must.

Granny
Eight years later, my mother's mother, my Granny, had a stroke. She had always asked that she not be kept alive if it was time for her to go Home, so we requested that the doctors only do what was necessary to keep her comfortable. Within a week, she was asking to be fed, so they put in a nasal tube, then later a stomach peg, through which to give her daily nutrition.

About three months later, as she was in the rehab facility, I was sitting with her as she did her therapy. She pointed to the peg and asked, "Why did you do this to me?" I wanted to cry, but I told her that she had asked them to feed her. Of course, she had no recollection of that. The look in her eyes gave me my marching orders, so I literally went to battle to get that peg removed for her, as she withdrew consent and refused further intervention. She was able to swallow a soft diet, so she was able to enjoy tasty meals again.

When she had another stroke a couple of months later, we were adamant about not prolonging her suffering, so we declined any IV, resuscitation or medication, besides those that would keep her comfortable. I had been at her bedside every single day for six months, making sure that she got the care she deserved and was at her bedside when she inhaled and exhaled for the last time. Her favorite hymn was "Because He Lives", so I sang it as she left us to go Home.

Mary

A couple of years before that, my mother-in-law, Mary, had been diagnosed with colon cancer. She chose surgery and chemo, which she handled like a champ. She beat that cancer back for several years and got to see the birth of several great grandbabies. She sure did love all her babies!

As I mentioned earlier, the day came that she didn't need to live alone, so we invited her to move in with us. Our house was laid out in such a way that she was able to take two bedrooms with a Jack and Jill bath between them, and convert one of the bedrooms into a living room to make her own living space. (I've already nominated my husband for sainthood, but here's another jewel in his crown: Steve has three sisters, but he wanted to take care of his momma. I really love that about him.)

Over the course of the two years she was with us, she had additional surgeries and treatments. The last two months of her life, all her children took turns being with her and providing her with love and care around the clock. As she was nearing the end of her journey here, she leaned up from her pillow, looked over at me and said, "I need you to pack my suitcase." I said, "Sugar, you don't need a suitcase where you're going." She seemed confused at first, then she relaxed as she laid back and said, "I guess that's right." A couple of days later, she breathed her last.

You've read that I saw my dad pass from this life, too. Watching the instant of death wasn't easy, but it was utterly fascinating. We're not made to stay here. Being a witness was a spectacular privilege.

One thing I learned in all these experiences was that I can be a bulldog to get something done for someone who cannot speak for themselves. The medical community is hard-wired to give drugs and perform procedures, for which I am thankful when they are used correctly. However, when it is time to let a saint go Home, family members must be bold enough to fulfill the wishes of their loved one. It is easier to tell the doctor, "Ok, do whatever you have to do," but if it isn't the wish of the patient, then it's a cop-out. I completely understand that the bold choices involve life and death, but it isn't my preference that my family would want to keep me here when my body is ready and my spirit is begging to go Home.

When Daddy was in ICU and recently off the ventilator, I told them that he didn't want to be on the ventilator again or have any other drastic measures taken, so we needed to sign a DNR (do not resuscitate) and a DNI (do not intubate). The nurse told me that was a brave decision, but three of his doctors came in and tried to talk him out of it by using all types of scary what-if scenarios. I was so proud of him as he listened politely then told them, "I'll take my chances."

In the few hours before he died, for a reason I didn't understand at the time, I reminded his nurses that he had a

DNR and a DNI. As I left that night, you may recall that I told him, "You know they are all telling me how you need to eat and drink more, but I'm not going to fight you on this. You do what you want. You *can* get better, so I will come tomorrow and do every step of your rehab beside you, and I will fight for you to get back to where you were. But, if this is what you want (pointing to him lying in bed), I will fight for you, and they will not put another tube in you."

I believe that he trusted me to protect him and honor his wishes, even though I certainly wasn't ready to have him leave. Grief is no leisurely walk in the park. It has no rules or time limits. We get to walk that path on our own terms at our own pace.

Yahweh is a name used for God and is sometimes spelled Yhwh. I've been told that Yahweh is literally the sound of our beginning and our end. A newborn inhales with a "yah", and the last breath leaving our lungs is "weh".

Try it. Breath in "Yah". Exhale "weh".

I've witnessed this accurate description of the sounds of birth and of death. Everything we are, from start to finish, *proclaims His name*. Wow. Just WOW.

Several of my friends have children who are in Heaven. One mommy said this, "I don't know why people refer to death as *losing* someone. My baby girl isn't *lost*. I know exactly where she is." That is such a pleasant thought. Her daughter is with the One who loves her most.

That's where I want to be, too.

These stories are not shared to make us all bawl, but death is not an option, so we know it's coming, yet we rarely get to exit on our terms. I share this in the hope of emboldening those who are caregivers and are faced with end-of-life choices for the one they love. If end-of-life wishes have been made known, please honor those wishes as your final act of true love.

Ok, now this poem may make you cry.

The Last Time

From the moment you hold your baby in your arms, you will never be the same.
You might long for the person you were before, when you had freedom and time, and nothing in particular to worry about.
You will know tiredness like you never knew it before, and days will run into days that are exactly the same, full of feedings and burping, nappy changes and crying, whining and fighting, naps or a lack of naps, it might seem like a never-ending cycle.

But don't forget...
There is a last time for everything.
There will come a time when you will feed your baby for the very last time.
They will fall asleep on you after a long day and it will be the last time you ever hold your sleeping child.

One day you will carry them on your hip, then set them
down, and never pick them up that way again.
You will scrub their hair in the bath one night
and from that day on they will want to bathe alone.
They will hold your hand to cross the road, then they will
never reach for it again.
They will creep into your room at midnight for cuddles,
and it will be the last time you ever wake to this.
One afternoon you will sing "the wheels on the bus" and do
all the actions, then never sing them that way again.
They will kiss you goodbye at the school gate,
then the next day they will ask to walk to the gate alone.
You will read a final bedtime story
and wipe your last dirty face.
They will one day run to you with arms raised,
for the very last time.
The thing is, you won't even know it's the last time
until there are no more times, and even then,
it will take you a while to realize.
So while you are living in these times,
remember there are only so many of them
and when they are gone,
you will yearn for just one more day of them.
For one last time.
--Author Unknown

Yes, I cried messy tears, knowing that every single word is true. I was reminded to cherish and relish the details of life well-lived and well-loved. We can be too busy (checking our smart phones), or we can choose to gently savor every single second.

Sitting by my dad's bedside as he was in the hospital, we had a chance to say what needed saying. However, when I visited with him for the last time, I didn't realize it was the last time I'd hear his voice. You can be sure that I am more aware of the moments I have left with my mother.

Moments.

Put Me in, Coach

There is a "death crawl" scene in the movie, *Facing The Giants*. It is my favorite movie scene of all time. (Go watch this movie now if you haven't seen it!)

When this film came out, I called one of my mentors and asked him to watch it. I said, "The acting isn't great, but the message is powerful. There is one scene that will take your breath away. You'll know when you get to it."

He called me later and said, "Yeah, as I started watching it, I wondered if you knew what you were talking about. But then, yeah, I got it."

Folks, I can't watch this incredible scene without my eyes leaking that familiar salty liquid. I can see God/Jesus/Holy Spirit on the ground beside me, urging me to not give up, to not quit, to keep moving until I have nothing left. He says, "I know it hurts, but keep going! You're almost there! Give me your very best!"

Folks, I know it hurts. I know you want to quit. Don't.

I've got more in me than I'm giving. I'm a disciple of Christ and others are watching me. If I act hopeless, others will not see the one true God in all His power and glory. My actions could dilute my influence or my God-given gifts.

It's a challenge. Life is full of challenges.

One of the grand benefits of getting older is that there is much experience to draw from each day. That's called "wisdom." Sometimes, it's comforting to know the correct answer for the crisis de jour; at other times, it's unsettling.

Have you ever felt like the huge, awful, terrible, unfair trial/crisis in front of you was just a training run, preparing you for something bigger? This is not a new feeling for me. For quite some time, I have felt that something is coming; a challenge that requires preparation.

Maybe, I've been preparing for this book that you're reading. (Thank you again, by the way.)

Maybe Jesus really meant it when He gave His disciples the Great Commission after His resurrection. Go and make disciples. It makes me uncomfortable because I doubt my ability to *go and make disciples*. Then, I feel guilty because I have the greatest gift of all time – eternal life – and I don't make it a priority to share that Good News with others.

Plus, the Holy Spirit's *unlimited power* is *within me*. I don't even pretend to understand this endowment. Some people do not know my Jesus and have no hope of Heaven. Maybe, that's what needed preparation – my heart - so that I would be bold enough to share the hope I have because He lives.

I have been dragging my feet and making excuses. Well, no more.

Twice in *Matthew*, the red letters of Jesus say, "the kingdom of heaven is near."

From that time on Jesus began to preach, "Repent, for the kingdom of heaven has come near." -- Matthew 4:17

As you go, proclaim this message: 'The kingdom of heaven has come near.' -- Matthew 10:7

Later in *Matthew 24*, more red letters of Jesus tell us to keep watch because He is coming back. Keep watch.

I've read the Old Testament book of *Esther* many times. (It's short, so please go read it as soon as you can.) The Lord will use whom He uses. Esther didn't want to be the one who had to stand up, but there was no other choice. Mordecai said, *"...if you remain silent at this time, relief and deliverance for the Jews will arise from another place, but you and your father's family will perish. And who knows but that you have come to royal position for such a time as this?"*

175

For such a time as this...

Sharlan Proper was my new friend in 1992. She was the first to quote that little phrase to me many years ago, as she helped me to seek my place in His Kingdom.

Esther was the right person in the right place at the right time. (Seriously, read the story. It's full of deceit, intrigue, beauty school, plot twists, and murder. It's fascinating!)

Maybe, I am the right person in the right place at the right time. Maybe I've been equipped to do what He asked me to do. Actually, I am sure of these things.

Folks, more often than not, we will find that we are the right person in the right place at the right time. God will use whom He uses. If we have chosen to be His willing followers, chances are pretty decent that He is using us right now to deliver His people.

So, _Philippians 1:27-28_ might be a New Testament epilog to Esther. _Whatever happens, conduct yourselves in a manner worthy of the gospel of Christ. Then ...I will know that you stand firm in the one Spirit, striving together as one for the faith of the gospel without being frightened in any way by those who oppose you. This is a sign to them that they will be destroyed, but that you will be saved—and that by God._

It's exciting to think that He would choose to use me for His kingdom! If He's still looking for someone imperfect, who makes a fair number of mistakes, but who loves Him, then

I'm the gal for this job. Seriously, the examples in The Book show that He chose plain folks to put His plans into motion, and I am plain folks.

Plus, I'm willing.

Open The Book. Be prepared. Keep watch. This is a training run. I can do my part by making sure that my heart is right so that He can put me in the right place at the right time.

Put me in. I'm ready!

But, God!

I'm not proud of all the sinful things I've said and done.

I've learned a lot in the past fifty-ish years, as I sought to be like Jesus. It seems to me that the first place to start is in His Word. If I am not taking the time to be in The Book, then I'm not equipping myself for the days ahead. Jesus came to Earth with a single purpose; to seek and save the lost. He didn't seek fortune or fame. He didn't get caught up in politics or the devil's schemes.

Through the years, I've found some lovely, wise friends who offer encouragement if I feel myself slipping down the slope of despair (and hysteria). I was desperately reaching out for a helping hand and one friend asked me to read *Ephesians*--all of it, in one sitting. I'd never read The Word like that before. Oh, how it blessed me then and continues to bless me today. Of course, I have had other moments through the years. I have read several of both Old and New Testament books in one sitting to gain their deeper message. My dear reader, when you have a few minutes, read the whole book of *Ephesians*, and then read *Philippians*. It's powerful stuff!

His message to us is always relevant. Always. If we never open the Word, we won't know what He has for us.

Reading the Word helps us personally, and it equips us to help others.

On one occasion an expert in the law stood up to test Jesus. "Teacher," he asked, "what must I do to inherit eternal life?" "What is written in the Law?" Jesus replied. "How do you read it?" He answered, "'Love the Lord your God with all your heart and with all your soul and with all your strength and with all your mind'; and, 'Love your neighbor as yourself.'" "You have answered correctly," Jesus replied. "Do this and you will live." –Luke 10:25-28

I would tell you that most of my life I loved the Lord my God with all my heart, with all my soul and with all my strength and with all my mind, but that isn't true. To the best of my recollection, I've always believed that Jesus is the Son of God, that He died on the cross for my sins, that He rose on the third day and that He lives today. The problems came Monday through Saturday when I lived like I wanted to live; making decisions that I wanted to make and saying what I wanted to say.

As the years have passed, I have come to love and trust Him more. I remember thinking that *I* knew what He wanted in my life. I ran as fast and hard toward my personal goals as possible. I was selfish and hurt a lot of people. I had a bad feeling in my stomach when I was not listening to Him, but I rationalized it and moved on to what *I* wanted. Every single time, those efforts failed. Now, when I get that bad feeling, I run the other way. Getting past "young and stupid" to arrive at "older and wiser" can be painful.

In *John 13*, Jesus is washing the disciples' feet. This made Peter uncomfortable. Jesus wanted his disciples to understand when he said, *"I have set you an example that you should do as I have done for you."*

Some of you may have had an experience with foot washing. Doing the washing is the easy part. Sitting there in complete resignation and accepting love is hard. Jesus knew that. He wanted us to learn to accept love because that brings us to a deeper awareness of giving love.

Easier said than done.

"My prayer for you today is not that you will like the sermon or be wowed by the music, but that you will have an encounter with God." -- Rick Atchley

Let that soak in for a moment. What does it even mean to *have an encounter with God*?

Maybe you see yourself as having sinned too much, falling too far for Jesus to want to save you. Maybe you can't imagine being as good as the person next to you. Your clothes aren't new or pressed or even all that clean. You've gained some weight so that dress is really too short or those slacks are too tight, but it's all you have. You only have flip flops. Your kids don't behave in the pew, and it's just exhausting to try to do this alone. You don't know what to say, and you sure can't sing. You hope no one talks to you. You're a gossip. You're an adulterer. You had sex before you got married. You had an abortion. You didn't breastfeed your babies. You've hit your wife and kids. You watch internet porn. You've cheated on your taxes. You're divorced. You were abused as a child. You're addicted to drugs or alcohol. You've been in jail.

Or maybe, we get caught up in *what's in it for me*. Are the pews comfortable? Is my favorite pew available? Can I visit with my friends instead of having to introduce myself to strangers? I sure hope no one does anything *weird* like clap or raise their holy hands. Should I listen to praise songs on the radio during the drive to the worship service? I hope no one says anything that will offend me.

Am I guilty of going to *church* and basically expecting to be upset by some thing or some one?

Good grief. I think I may have missed the point. Maybe, just maybe, God wants me to entrust my moments to Him, *every* moment.

Oh, yeah...
--Whatever, Lord. Whatever
--I am fearfully and wonderfully made
--For God so *loved* the world, that He gave his only son so that I might have eternal life
--forgive as I have been forgiven
--remove the plank in my own eye

--go and sin no more
--count myself dead to sin but alive to God in Christ Jesus
--the world will know I belong to God if I love others
--He is the Way, the Truth and the Life
--Therefore, go and make disciples of all nations, baptizing them in the name of the Father and of the Son and of the Holy Spirit, and teaching them to obey everything He has commanded. And surely He is with me always, to the very end of the age.

Love one another.
But, God! Do you know what he did?
Love one another.
But God! Do you know what she said?
Love one another.
But God! Do you know what I've done? What I've said?
I love you.
But God! BUT!!
I Love You.

We are begging for grace. Everyone around us is begging for grace. Why then, do we find it so difficult to offer grace? Why are we so quick to judge and so slow to love?

We can't possibly know what the Lord has asked the person sitting beside us to bear. On the next trip to the grocery (or hardware) store, let's turn and look around for a moment. Every person we see is fighting a battle that we know nothing about. It might seem like a good idea to be kind and show some compassion. Always.

What if we let the love of Christ dwell in our hearts? We know *that out of the overflow of the heart, the mouth speaks (Luke 6:45)*, so if we have made a cozy place for Jesus in our hearts, maybe our mouths would have loving and compassionate words for our sisters and brothers.

My favorite adult Bible teacher, Jeff Ray, would quote Adam Lindsay Gordon*: "Life is mostly froth and bubble, two things stand like stone, kindness in another's trouble and courage in your own."*

My favorite Savior says, *"By this everyone will know that you are my disciples if you love one another."*

Yes, I pray that we will have an encounter with God today.

Prayer: Father, in the name of Jesus, please forgive our petty squabbles, our selfish rants. Your children are the ones who should be showing your love, and we can't even love one another inside your family, your spiritual kingdom. Please prick our hearts so that we can clearly see you and your love. Please help me remove the gigantic plank from my own eye: the selfishness and unforgiving spirit and help me discern whatever is true and noble and right and pure and lovely so that I can think upon such things. You are my Lord and My God.

Outrageous Love
Extravagant Grace
Boundless Joy

Everything within me cries out to glorify Him with all that I am. His abiding and everlasting love astonishes me. His holiness surrounds me.

The story of the Cross tells of the incomprehensible depth and power of His love for His children. I have an opportunity and an obligation to build relationships so that others see Him in me.

I can show Him to the frazzled mom in the line at the grocery store or to the snippy cashier.

I can show Him to the guy who is too busy talking on his phone to drive safely.

I can show Him to my employer when I do my job with joy and seek to foster harmony in my office.

I can show Him to the waitress or waiter that didn't get my order exactly right by tipping anyway.

(Speaking of tipping those who serve us in a restaurant - It is said that the wait staff at many restaurants do not care to work on Sundays because of all the CATs that come in for lunch - Christians Against Tipping. I was appalled to hear this! Of all guests, we should be the most generous. To hear that we are the stingiest hurts my heart. We can do better, can't we?)

I can show Him every day and in every way. I can bless those around me. May I be aware of the open doors and never fall into my old patterns that shut those doors.

Please don't misread or misinterpret my message. I have been guilty of haughtily quoting chapter and verse instead of sitting down and embracing with compassion first, then teaching in humility. I don't claim to understand His ways, but here's what I read:

Flee also youthful lusts; but pursue righteousness, faith, love, peace with those who call on the Lord out of a pure heart. But avoid foolish and ignorant disputes, knowing that they generate strife. And a servant of the Lord must not quarrel but be gentle to all, able to teach, patient, in humility correcting those who are in opposition, if God perhaps will grant them repentance, so that they may know the truth, and that they may come to their senses and escape the snare of the devil, having been taken captive by him to do his will. --2 Timothy 2:22-26 (NKJV)

This passage brings to mind some issues I've seen on Facebook that seem to polarize the masses. The righteous ones start beating their chests while haughtily and vigorously quoting chapter and verse, creating a quarrel. That sure makes folks want to sit down for a neighborly Bible study, doesn't it?

Preach the word; be prepared in season and out of season; correct, rebuke and encourage—with great patience and careful instruction. For the time will come when people will not put up with sound doctrine. Instead, to suit their own desires, they will gather around them a great number of teachers to say what their itching ears want to hear. They will turn their ears away from the truth and turn aside to myths. -- 2 Timothy 4: 2-4

I have had *itching ears* on my heart for some time now, as you may have read on my blog. If we're gonna sin, let's be honest that we're just selfish and want to do it our way, not His way. He is a loving God, no doubt, but He won't be mocked. Sin is always sin. Just because our culture accepts it and just because Jesus loves us anyway, doesn't mean that it doesn't break His heart and that we will have some 'splaining to do (cue Ricky Ricardo).

A transformed life is self-evident. A life controlled by the Spirit *knows* the chapter and verse, but doesn't use it as a weapon. I'll never convince someone that Jesus is Lord of my life if I don't meet them where they are and show them His love. Again, I consider: *They will know you are my disciples if you love one another.*

As I said earlier, I serve at the pleasure of The King. He asks each one of us to feed His sheep. What will we do? How will we be His hands and feet? You may be asking yourself, "Is this lady crazy? She's talking about loving and forgiving and being thankful. She's a bossy one. She has no idea what my personal circumstances are."

You're right. I don't. But the Lord of the Universe, the King of Kings and the Lord of Lords, the great I Am, the Prince of Peace...does know.

Trust in the Lord with all your heart and lean not on your own understanding; in all your ways submit to him, and he will make your paths straight. -- Proverbs 3:5-6

That's what we need: straight paths, a steady hand. Trust Him. Trust the pattern He gave us. Trust His timing. Trust His power.

Maybe you have heard this quote: "Only God can turn a test into a testimony, a mess into a message, a trial into a triumph and a victim into a victory." *Believe it.*

We all have pieces of our lives that don't seem to fit with other pieces of our lives. If the Instruction Manual (Bible) tells us *what* and *how,* maybe we should trust it. If it just doesn't make sense or if we just don't like how the instructions tell us to do it, maybe we should trust the instructions anyway.

I've done some cross stitching in my life. Back when our little ones took naps, I actually had time to sit down long enough to complete a piece of needlework. The front of it is perfect. The stitches are placed on the right squares, per the pattern. It becomes a piece of artwork that is worthy of being framed and displayed.

But a quick glance at the back of the fabric tells another story. The beautiful design is not discernable when viewed from the underside. It's confusing and misunderstood.

We bring our bucket of *stuff* to God: faded scraps of shame, threads of doubt, cords of fear and needles of unforgiveness. He can (and will) create an extravagantly beautiful work of art in you and me, to be used for His good purpose. In Him, we are *enough*. We are children of The King, dearly loved, just like we are.

Let's get out in the world and share grace and offer courage to those who cannot imagine being *enough*; women and men that we come into contact with each day who are literally dying to know that someone loves them and accepts them, just as they are. May our hearts and our arms be wide open to receive whoever He sends our way. We don't need to be snooty church folks who look down their noses, then huff and puff their disapproval with a sanctimonious flair.

Do you remember Ray Stevens' song, "The Mississippi Squirrel Revival" and Sister Bertha Better-Than-You, who sat down front in the Amen Pew of the First Self-Righteous Church? (Its well-worth your time to listen to it.)

We need to not be like her.

We can be the hands and feet of Jesus when we embrace the ones that He sends into our path, and then we love them enough to refuse to leave them the way we find them. We show them how to be just like Jesus. And, maybe, just maybe, they can show us a thing or two about how to be just like Jesus, too.

And Jabez called on the God of Israel saying, "Oh, that You would bless me indeed, and enlarge my territory, that Your hand would be with me, and that You would keep me from evil, that I may not cause pain!" So God granted him what he requested. -- 1 Chronicles 4:10 (NKJV)

I've prayed over and over again that part about "please keep me from evil that I may not cause pain." I have made so many mistakes and hurt so many people through the years. It grieves me that I have acted in such a way as to give others the wrong impression of my Lord. I wish I could turn back the hands of time and, at least, fix those moments. But, alas, I cannot. What's done is done. I've repented, and now, it's time to move on and do better, as I am aware of what is at stake.

"People are like stained-glass windows. They sparkle and shine when the sun is out, but when the darkness sets in,

their true beauty is revealed only if there is a light from within." – Dr. Elisabeth Kubler Ross

I can offer others grace and courage as I show them love, which is really just His love, shining through me. I'm still working to drop my old habit of looking at outward appearance first. Please don't give up on me!

Dear friends, let us love one another, for love comes from God. Everyone who loves has been born of God and knows God. Whoever does not love does not know God, because God is love. This is how God showed his love among us: He sent his one and only Son into the world that we might live through him. This is love: not that we loved God, but that he loved us and sent his Son as an atoning sacrifice for our sins. Dear friends, since God so loved us, we also ought to love one another. No one has ever seen God; but if we love one another, God lives in us and his love is made complete in us. -- 1 John 4:7-12

I want God to live in me and for His love to be complete in me. I'm not there yet, but I'm marching in that direction. If we will spend more time with God in His word, seek His blessings and recognize that He is faithful in keeping His promises, He'll meet us there.

I hope you're inspired to seek Him more, love more and be more for His Kingdom.

Did you hear me say "do more"?

NO!

I hope to inspire you to <u>*seek Him*</u> more, <u>*love*</u> more and <u>*be*</u> more for His Kingdom as you show outrageous love, extravagant grace, and boundless joy!

God bless you as you journey with Him. I hope to see you down the road.

Until We Meet Again

My prayers for you:

For this reason I kneel before the Father, from whom every family in heaven and on earth derives its name. I pray that out of his glorious riches he may strengthen you with power through his Spirit in your inner being, so that Christ may dwell in your hearts through faith. And I pray that you, being rooted and established in love, may have power, together with all the Lord's holy people, to grasp how wide and long and high and deep is the love of Christ, and to know this love that surpasses knowledge—that you may be filled to the measure of all the fullness of God.
Now to him who is able to do immeasurably more than all we ask or imagine, according to his power that is at work within us, to him be glory in the church and in Christ Jesus throughout all generations, for ever and ever! Amen.
-- Ephesians 3:14-21

The LORD bless you and keep you;
the LORD make his face shine on you
and be gracious to you;
the LORD turn his face toward you and give you peace.
-- Numbers 6:24-26

About the Author

Carrie Blair is a business owner and a Bible teacher who has a passion for sharing her personal life stories through her blog and speaking engagements. She and her husband, Stephen, also work together as Aflac agents. They live in Lubbock, Texas, where Carrie can be found writing, singing and sneaking a bite of prescription-strength dark chocolate at every opportunity.

Do you want to contact Carrie about booking a faith, motivational or professional presentation? You can find her online press page here:
www.carrieblair.net/press-kit

You can read Carrie's blog at www.carrieblair.net

Carrie and Stephen are working together on a book about their marriage and professional journey, so be looking for We're All In!

www.ingramcontent.com/pod-product-compliance
Lightning Source LLC
Chambersburg PA
CBHW072001040426
42447CB00009B/1431